NINJA FOODI SMART XL GRILL COOKBOOK #2021

New Tasty & Delicious Recipes For Indoor Grilling & Air Frying Perfection

BY

Elizabeth Presley

ASIN: 978-1-63810-011-9

COPYRIGHT © 2021 by Elizabeth Presley

All rights reserved. This book is copyright protected and it's for personal use only. Without the prior written permission of the publisher, no part of this publication should be reproduced, distributed, or transmitted in any form or by any means, including photocopying, recording, or other electronic or mechanical methods.

This publication is sold with the idea that the publisher is not required to render accounting, officially permitted, or otherwise, qualified services. If advice is required, it is necessary to seek the services of a legal or professional, a practiced individual in the profession. This document is geared towards providing substantial and reliable information in regards to the topics covered.

DISCLAIMER

The information written in this book is for educational and entertainment purposes only. Strenuous efforts have been made to provide accurate, up to date and reliable complete information. The information in this book is true and complete to the best of our knowledge. All recommendations are made without guarantee on the part of the author and publisher.

Neither the publisher nor the author takes any responsibility for any possible consequences of reading or enjoying the recipes in this book. The author and publisher disclaim any liability in connection with the use of information contained in this book. Under no circumstance will any legal responsibility or blame be apportioned against the author or publisher for any reparation, damages, or monetary loss due to the information herein, either directly or indirectly.

Table of Contents

INTRODUCTION 7
   What is Ninja Foodi Smart XL Grill 7
Getting To Know The Ninja Foodi Smart XL Grill 8
   Function Buttons 8
   Operating Buttons 8
Cleaning Your Ninja Foodi Smart XL Grill 9
Troubleshooting Tips 11

BREAKFAST RECIPES 13
   Hash Brown Casserole 13
   Bacon and Egg 14
   Asparagus and Cheese Strata 15
   Broccoli Quiche 16
   Egg and Avocado Burrito 17
   Breakfast Sausages 18
   Brown Rice Porridge with Coconut Milk 19
   Fried Potatoes 20
   Western Omelet 21
   Breakfast Casserole 22
   Sausage and Cheese Quiche 23
   Pumpkin Egg Bake 24
   Spinach with Scrambled Eggs 25

BEEF & PORK RECIPES 26
   Beef Schnitzel 26
   Grilled Flank Steak 27
   Baby Back Ribs 28
   Lamb Chops with Rosemary 29
   Korean BBQ Beef 30
   Teriyaki Pork Ribs 31
   Beef Meatballs 32
   Pork Tenderloin 33

Lamb Ribs 34

Korean-Style Steak Tips 35

POULTRY RECIPES 36

Mayonnaise-Mustard Chicken 36

Roasted Cajun Turkey 37

Lime Chicken with Cilantro 38

Cajun Turkey 39

Chicken Breast 40

Asian Turkey Meatballs 41

Spicy BBQ Chicken Drumsticks 42

Turkey Meatloaves 43

Turkey Tenderloin 44

Teriyaki Chicken Wings 45

Turkey Bell Peppers 46

Sweet and Sour Turkey Meatballs 47

Chicken Thighs 48

VEGAN & VEGETARIAN 49

Roasted Garlic and Asparagus 49

Cheese Stuffed Vegetable 50

Kidney Beans Oatmeal 51

Brussel Sprouts 52

Rosemary Potatoes 53

Italian Tofu 54

Cabbage and Red Pepper Flakes 55

Spicy Broccoli with Parmesan 56

Acorn Squash 57

Roasted Ratatouille 58

BEEF & PORK RECIPES 59

Breaded Scallops 59

Beef Schnitzel 60

Lamb Ribs 61

Pork Chops 62

Pork Tenderloin 63

Flank Steak 64

Korean BBQ Beef 65

Baby Back Ribs 66

Lamb Chops with Rosemary 67

Beef Meatballs 68

Pork Meatballs 69

Teriyaki Pork Ribs 70

Pork Sausage 71

Vietnamese Pork Chops 72

FISH & SEAFOOD RECIPES 73

Coconut Chili Fish Curry 73

Paprika Shrimp 74

Shrimp Tacos 75

Crab Ratatouille 76

Shrimp and Vegetable Paella 77

Cod Fillet with Sesame Seeds 78

Fish Tacos 79

Salmon Patty Bites 80

Orange Shrimp 81

Cod Fingers 82

APPETIZER RECIPES 83

Air Fried Potatoes 83

Steak Fries 84

Sweet Potato Chips 85

BBQ Chicken Pizza 86

Cheese Sandwiches 87

Prosciutto-Wrapped Asparagus 88

Kale Chips 89

Cheesy Artichoke 90

French Fries 91

DESSERT RECIPES 92

Chocolate S'mores 92

Apple Crisp 93

Lemon Ricotta Cake 94

Chocolate Bread Pudding 95

Chia Pudding 96

Cinnamon Candied Apples 97

Chocolate Pecan Pie 98

Coconut Chocolate Cake 99

Blueberry Cobbler 100

INTRODUCTION

Are you looking for delicious and effortless recipes to take advantage of the amazing versatility of your Ninja Foodi Smart XL Grill?

If this is what you are looking for then keep reading...

The Ninja Foodi Smart XL Grill delivers your perfect doneness without the guesswork.

In addition, as you know, this amazing appliance is the perfect companion in the kitchen, both for large families, for anyone who wants to grill indoor without losing the outdoor grill taste, and for anyone who want to air fry for eat crispy and crunchy food with guilt-free.

The Ninja Foodi Smart XL Grill is the Smart XL grill that sears, sizzles, and air fry crisps. It possesses an XL capacity and innovative Smart Cook System, grill even more and reaches your desired doneness with the touch of a button. It's also an air fry crisper so you can enjoy your favorite guilt-free fried foods.

Perfectly cook food on the inside to your desired doneness and char grill every side with 500F Cyclonic Grilling Technology and the Smart Cook System. 500F cyclonic air and the 500F grill grate combine to give you delicious char-grilled marks and flavors. It has a Smart Cook System—4 smart protein settings, 9 customizable doneness levels, and the Foodi Smart Thermometer enable you to achieve the perfect doneness with the touch of a button. They can be used to grill 50% more food than the original Ninja Foodi Grill for delicious family sized meals. It is versatile and grills your favorite foods to char grilled perfection, or go beyond grilling with 5 additional cooking functions: Air Crisp, Bake, Roast, Broil, and Dehydrate

What is Ninja Foodi Smart XL Grill

As the name suggests, Ninja Foodi Smart XL Grill can be used to air crisp, bake, roast, broil and dehydrate your favorite food with the touch of a button. It air fry crisps with up to 75% less fat than deep frying using the crisper basket. The versatility of the grill, saying the "air crisp function allows you to emulate deep frying without the large amount of oil.

The grill function by type of meat is awesome especially with the thermometer. It allows you to select how cooked you want your meat and have no smoke. It's the perfect time to grab this multitasking wonder.

Getting To Know The Ninja Foodi Smart XL Grill

Function Buttons

GRILL: Grill indoors while creating even char, grill marks, and grilled flavor.

AIR CRISP: For crispiness and crunch with little to no oil.

BAKE: Bake cakes, treats, desserts, and more.

ROAST: Tenderize meats, roast vegetables, and more.

DEHYDRATE: Dehydrate meats, fruits, and vegetables for healthy snacks.

BROIL: Add the crispy finishing touch to meals or melt cheese on sandwiches.

Operating Buttons

POWER button: The power button can be used to turn on the unit once the unit is plugged in. Pressing it during cooking stops the current cooking function and turns off the unit.

Left arrows: Use the up and down arrows to the left of the display to adjust the cooking temperature in any function or to set the internal doneness when using PRESET and MANUAL buttons.

Right arrows: Use the up and down arrows to the right of the display to set the food type when using PRESET or to adjust the cook time when not cooking with the Foodi Smart Thermometer.

MANUAL button: This button can be used to switch the display screen to manually set the thermometer internal doneness. Manual button does not work with Dehydrate function.

PRESET button: Switches the display screen so you can set the thermometer, food type, and internal doneness based on the preset temperatures. Preset button does not work with Dehydrate function. Press the up and down arrows to adjust the temperature or time during cooking. The unit will then resume at those settings.

START/STOP button: After selecting temperature and time, press the START/STOP button to start cooking.

Standby Mode: The unit usually goes into standby mode when there's no interaction with the control panel for 10 minutes and the unit is not cooking.

Preheat: Once the unit is preheating, it will be observed by a progress bar on the display screen and the PREHEAT button will illuminate. To turn off Preheat, press the PREHEAT button while the grill is in preheat state. ADD FOOD will display

Cleaning Your Ninja Foodi Smart XL Grill

The unit should be cleaned thoroughly after every use. Always let the appliance cool before cleaning.

1. Unplug the unit from the wall outlet before cleaning. Leave the hood open after transfer your food to a serving bowl to let the unit cool quicker.

2. The cooking pot, grill grate, crisper basket, splatter shield, cleaning brush, and any other included accessories are dishwasher safe, except the thermometer. DO NOT place the thermometer in the dishwasher.

3. For the best dishwasher cleaning results, you have to rinse the grill grate, crisper basket, splatter shield, and any other accessories with warm water before placing them in the dishwasher.

4. If hand-washing, you can use cleaning brush to wash the parts. Use the opposite end of the cleaning brush to scrap off any browned bits that's stuck to the unit. Air-dry or pat dry with a paper towel after hand-washing.
   DO NOT use liquid cleaning solution on or near the thermometer jack. Use a compressed air or a cotton swab to avoid damaging the jack.

5. When any food residue or grease are stuck on the grill grate, splatter shield, or any other removable part, soak in warm soapy water before cleaning.

6. Clean the splatter shield after every use. Soaking the splatter shield for a couple of minutes or hours can help soften the baked-on grease.

7. After soaking, use the cleaning brush to remove the grease from the stainless-steel frame and front tabs.

8. Deep clean the splatter shield by placing it in a pot of water and boiling it for about 10 minutes to soften the residue or grease. Rinse with room temperature water and allow to dry completely.

9. To deep clean the thermometer, soak the stainless-steel tip and silicone grip in warm, soapy water. DO NOT immerse the cord or jack in water or any other liquid.

10. The Foodi Smart Thermometer holder is handwash only. DO NOT use abrasive tools or cleaners. NEVER immerse the main unit in water or any other liquid.

Troubleshooting Tips

1. **"Add Food" appears on the control panel display.**

The unit has preheated already and its time to add the ingredients to be cooked.

2. **"Shut Lid" appears on the control panel display.**

The hood is open and needs to be closed for the selected function to start.

3. **"Plug In" appears on the control panel display.**

It means that the thermometer is not plugged into the jack on the right side of the control panel. Plug the thermometer in before proceeding. Press the thermometer in until you hear a click.

4. **"PRBE ERR" appears on the control panel display.**

This happens when the unit timed out before food reached the set internal temperature. As a protection for the unit, it can run for only certain lengths of time at specific temperatures.

5. **"E" appears on the control panel display.**

The unit is not functioning properly. You can Contact Customer Service for further assistance.

6. **Why is my food overcooked or undercooked even though I used the thermometer?**

It is vital to insert the thermometer lengthwise into the thickest part of the ingredient to get the most accurate reading.

7. **Why does the preheat progress bar not start from the beginning?**

When the unit is warm from previously being used, it will not require the full preheating time.

8. **Can I cancel or override preheating?**

Preheating is highly recommended for accurate results, but you can omit it by selecting the PREHEAT button after you press the START/STOP button.

9. **Should I add my ingredients before or after preheating?**

Allow the unit to preheat before adding your ingredients.

10. **Why is my unit emitting smoke?**

When using the Grill function, always select the recommended temperature setting.

11. How do I pause the unit so I can check my food?

When the hood is opened during a cooking function, the unit will automatically pause.

12. Will the thermometer grip melt if it touches the hot grill grate?

No, the grip is made of a high-temperature silicone that can handle the Ninja Foodi Smart XL Grill's high temperatures.

13. My food is burned.

Never add your ingredients until recommended preheat time is complete. Always check the progress throughout cooking, and remove food when desired level of brownness has reached. Transfer the food to serving bowl immediately after the cook time is complete to avoid overcooking.

14. Why did a circuit breaker trip while using the unit?

The unit uses 1760 watts of power, so it is absolutely important to be plugged into an outlet on a 15-amp circuit breaker. An outlet of 10-amp breaker will lead to the breaker to trip. The unit should be the only appliance plugged into an outlet when in use.

15. Why does the unit have a 1–9 scale for the Beef Preset?

The 1–9 scale provides a wide range of options for each doneness level so you can customize doneness to your liking.

BREAKFAST RECIPES
Hash Brown Casserole

Preparation time: 10 minutes

Cook time: 30 minutes

Total time: 40 minutes

Serves: 4

Ingredients:

- 1 (10.5-oz) can cream of chicken soup
- ½ cup sour cream
- 1 cup of minced onion
- ½ cup of shredded sharp Cheddar cheese
- 3 ½ cups frozen hash browns, thawed
- 1 tsp. salt
- 1 tsp. freshly ground black pepper
- 3 tbsp. butter, melted

Cooking Instructions:

1. In a medium bowl, add the hash browns and season with salt and black pepper. Add the melted butter.

2. Add the cream of chicken soup, and sour cream and give everything a good stir to combine. Mix in the minced onion and cheese and stir well.

3. Press the BAKE function, set the temperature to 325°F (163°C), and set the time for 30 minutes. Press the START/ STOP function to start preheating.

4. Take a cooking spray to spray a baking pan and arrange the hash brown mixture evenly into the baking pan. Transfer the baking pan into the pot.

5. Seal the hood and BAKE for 30 minutes until browned. Allow to cool for a couple of minutes before serving.

6. Serve and enjoy!

Bacon and Egg

Preparation time: 15 minutes

Cook time: 12 minutes

Total time: 27 minutes

Serves: 4

Ingredients:

- 5 eggs
- 2 tbsp. heavy cream
- 3 strips precooked bacon, chopped
- 4 (3-by-4-inch) crusty rolls
- 4 thin slices Gouda or Swiss cheese mini wedges
- ½ tsp. dried thyme
- Dash of salt
- Freshly ground black pepper, to taste

Cooking Instructions:

1. Press the BAKE function, set the temperature to 330°F (166°C), and set the time to 12 minutes. Press the START/STOP function to start preheating.

2. Place the rolls on a chopping board and cut off the tops. Remove the inside of the rolls with your fingers and form bread cups, leaving a ½-inch shell.

3. Add a slice of cheese onto each roll bottom. In a medium bowl, combine together the eggs and heavy cream until incorporated.

4. Add the bacon, thyme, salt, and pepper and give everything a good stir. Spoon the egg mixture into the prepared bread cups.

5. Transfer the bread cups into the pot. Seal the hood and BAKE for 10 to 12 minutes, or until the eggs are cooked through.

6. Serve hot and enjoy!

Asparagus and Cheese Strata

Preparation time: 15 minutes

Cook time: 19 minutes

Total time: 34 minutes

Serves: 4

Ingredients:

- 4 eggs
- 3 tbsp. whole milk
- 2 tbsp. chopped flat-leaf parsley
- 6 asparagus spears, cut into 2-inch pieces
- 1 tbsp. water
- 2 slices whole-wheat bread, cut into ½-inch cubes
- ½ cup grated Havarti or Swiss cheese
- Salt, to taste
- Freshly ground black pepper, to taste

Cooking Instructions:

1. Press the BAKE function, set the temperature to 330°F (166°C), and set the time to 19 minutes. Press the START/STOP to start preheating.

2. In a baking pan, dump the asparagus spears along with 1 tbsp. of water. Transfer the baking pan into the pot.

3. Seal the hood and BAKE for 4 to 5 minutes or until tender. Take out the asparagus from the pan and pat dry with paper towels.

4. Spray the pan with cooking spray. Add the bread and asparagus in the baking pan. In a medium bowl, combine together the eggs and milk until creamy.

5. Add the parsley, cheese, salt, and pepper and give everything a good stir to combine. Pour this mixture into the baking pan.

6. Transfer the pan into the pot and lock the hood. BAKE for 11 to 14 minutes, or until the eggs are browned. Allow to cool for a couple of before slicing and serving.

7. Serve immediately and enjoy!

Broccoli Quiche

Preparation time: 10 minutes

Cook time: 10 minutes

Total time: 20 minutes

Serves: 4

Ingredients:

- 6 eggs, beaten
- ¾ cup of heavy cream
- 1 cup of broccoli florets
- ¾ cup of chopped roasted red peppers
- 1 ¼ cups of grated Fontina cheese
- ½ tsp. salt
- Freshly ground black pepper, to taste

Cooking Instructions:

1. Press the AIR CRISP function, set the temperature to 325°F (163°C), and set the time for 10 minutes. Start preheating by pressing the START/STOP button.

2. Take a cooking spray to spray a baking pan. Add the broccoli florets and roasted red peppers to the pan. Arrange the grated Fontina cheese on top.

3. Beat the eggs in a mixing bowl and add the heavy cream. Season with salt and pepper. Pour the egg mixture over the top of the cheese.

4. Cover the baking pan with a piece of foil. Transfer the pan into pot and seal the hood. Select the AIR CRISP function for 8 minutes.

5. Take out the foil and cook for additional 2 minutes or until the quiche turns golden brown. Allow to cool for a couple of minutes before cutting into wedges.

6. Serve hot and enjoy!

Egg and Avocado Burrito

Preparation time: 15 minutes

Cook time: 5 minutes

Total time: 20 minutes

Serves: 4

Ingredients:

- 4 low-sodium whole-wheat flour tortillas

Filling Ingredients:

- 1 hard-boiled egg, chopped
- 2 hard-boiled egg whites, chopped
- 1 ripe avocado, peeled, and chopped
- 1 red bell pepper, chopped
- 1 (1.2-oz.) slice low-sodium, low-fat American cheese, torn into pieces
- 3 tbsp. low-sodium salsa, optional

Cooking Instructions:

1. Place the Crisper Basket into the Ninja Foodi Grill and seal the hood. Press the AIR CRISP function and set the temperature to 390°F (199°C).

2. Set it for 5 minutes. Start preheating by pressing the START/STOP function.

3. To make the filling: Add together the egg, egg whites, avocado, red bell pepper, cheese, and salsa in a medium bowl. Give everything a good stir to combine.

4. Place the tortillas on a chopping board and add ¼ of the prepared filling in the middle of each tortilla, leaving about 1 ½-inch on each end unfilled.

5. Slowly wrap up the opposite sides of each tortilla and roll up. Place the burritos to the Crisper Basket and seal the hood.

6. Select the AIR CRISP function for 4 to 5 minutes, or until the burritos turns golden brown. Let to rest for a couple of minutes.

7. Serve with salsa, if desired and enjoy!

Breakfast Sausages

Preparation time: 10 minutes

Cook time: 12 minutes

Total time: 22 minutes

Serves: 8 patties

Ingredients:

- 1 lb. ground chicken breast
- 1 egg white
- 1/3 cup of minced onion
- 3 tbsp. ground almonds
- 1 Granny Smith apple, peeled and chopped
- 2 tbsp. apple juice
- 2 garlic cloves, minced
- ⅛ tsp. freshly ground black pepper

Cooking Instructions:

1. Place the Crisper Basket into the Ninja Foodi Grill and seal the hood. Press the AIR CRISP function and set the temperature to 330°F (166°C).

2. Set if to 12 minutes. Select START/ STOP to begin preheating. In a medium bowl, add together all the ingredients except the chicken.

3. Give everything a good stir. Add the chicken breast to the apple mixture and mix everything until well incorporated.

4. Divide the mixture into 8 equal portions and shape into patties. Arrange the patties in the Crisper Basket. Seal the hood and select the AIR CRISP function.

5. Cook for 8 to 12 minutes, or until a meat thermometer inserted in the center of the chicken reaches at least 165°F (74°C).

6. Remove from the grill to a bowl and repeat with the remaining patties. Allow the chicken to cool for a couple of minutes.

7. Serve hot and enjoy!

Brown Rice Porridge with Coconut Milk

Preparation time: 10 minutes

Cook time: 23 minutes

Total time: 33 minutes

Serves: 1

Ingredients:

- 2 ½ cup cooked brown rice
- 4 large Medjool dates, pitted and chopped
- ½ tsp. kosher salt
- 1 cup canned coconut milk
- ¼ cup unsweetened shredded coconut
- ¼ cup packed dark brown sugar
- ¼ tsp. ground cardamom Heavy cream, optional if desired

Cooking Instructions:

1. Click the BAKE function and set the temperature to 375°F and set the time to 23 minutes. Press the START/STOP function to start preheating.

2. Add all the ingredients except the heavy cream in a baking pan and give everything a good stir until blended.

3. Transfer the baking pan into the pot. Seal the hood and BAKE for 23 minutes until the porridge is thick and creamy.

4. Stir the porridge midway through the cooking. Remove from the grill and spoon the porridge into serving plates.

5. Serve warm with a drizzle of the cream, if desired.

Fried Potatoes

Preparation time: 15 minutes

Cook time: 35 minutes

Total time: 50 minutes

Serves: 4

Ingredients:

- 1 lb. red potatoes, cut into ½-inch dices
- 1 large red bell pepper, cut into ½-inch dices
- 1 large green bell pepper, cut into ½-inch dices
- 1 small onion, cut into ½-inch dices
- 1½ tbsp. extra-virgin olive oil
- 1¼ tsp. kosher salt
- ¾ tsp. sweet paprika
- ¾ tsp. garlic powder
- Freshly ground black pepper, to taste

Cooking Instructions:

1. Insert the Crisper Basket and close the hood. Select AIR CRISP, set the temperature to 350°F (177°C), and set the time to 35 minutes.

2. Select START/STOP to start preheating. In a medium bowl, combine together the potatoes, bell peppers, onion, oil, salt, paprika, garlic powder, and black pepper.

3. Toss the ingredients to coat. Place the potato mixture to the Crisper Basket. Close the hood and AIR CRISP for 35 minutes, or until the potatoes are browned.

4. Shake the basket midway through the cooking. Remove from the basket to a serving bowl.

5. Serve warm and enjoy!

Western Omelet

Preparation time: 10 minutes

Cook time: 18 to 21 minutes

Total time: 31 minutes

Serves: 2

Ingredients:

- ¾ cup shredded sharp Cheddar cheese
- ¼ cup chopped bell pepper, green or red
- ¼ cup chopped onion
- ¼ cup diced ham
- 1 tsp. butter
- 4 eggs, beaten
- 2 tbsp. milk
- ⅛ tsp. salt

Cooking Instructions:

1. Select AIR CRISP, set the temperature to 390°F (199°C), and set the time to 6 minutes. Select START/STOP to start preheating.

2. In a baking pan, add together bell pepper, onion, ham, and butter. Give the ingredients a good mix. Place the pan directly in the pot.

3. Close the hood and AIR CRISP for 1 minute. Stir and cook for more 4 to 5 minutes until the veggies are softened.

4. In a medium bowl, whisk together the eggs, milk, and salt. Pour the egg mixture over the veggie mixture.

5. Reduce the grill temperature to 360°F (182°C) and BAKE for 13 to 15 minutes or until the top turn brown and the eggs are set.

6. Spread the omelet with the shredded cheese. Bake for additional 1 minute or until the cheese has dissolved.

7. Allow to cool for a couple of minutes before serving.

8. Serve and enjoy!

Breakfast Casserole

Preparation time: 10 minutes

Cook time: 17 to 19 minutes

Total time: 29 minutes

Serves: 4

Ingredients:

- 4 eggs, beaten
- 1 cup milk
- Salt, to taste
- Pepper, to taste
- 12 oz. ground chicken sausage
- 1 lb. frozen tater tots, thawed
- ¾ cup grated Cheddar cheese
- Cooking spray

Cooking Instructions:

1. In a medium bowl, whisk together the eggs and milk. Season with salt and pepper to taste and stir until mixed. Set aside.

2. Place a skillet over medium-high heat and spray with cooking spray. Add the ground sausage in the skillet and break it up into bite sizes a spoon.

3. Cook for 3 to 4 minutes or until the sausage starts to brown, stirring occasionally. Remove from heat and set aside.

4. Select BAKE, set the temperature to 400°F (204°C), and set the time to 15 minutes. Select START/STOP to start preheating.

5. Spray a baking pan with cooking spray. Place the tater tots in the baking pan. Place the pan directly in the pot. Close the hood and BAKE for 15 minutes.

6. Stir in the egg mixture and cooked sausage. Bake for additional 6 minutes. Spread the cheese on top of the tater tots.

7. Bake for additional 2 to 3 minutes or until the cheese is melted. Allow the mixture to cool for a couple of minutes before serving.

8. Serve and enjoy!

Sausage and Cheese Quiche

Preparation time: 10 minutes

Cook time: 25 minutes

Total time: 35 minutes

Serves: 4

Ingredients:

- 12 oz. sugar-free breakfast sausage
- 2 cups shredded Cheddar cheese
- 12 large eggs
- 1 cup heavy cream
- Salt, to taste
- Black pepper, to taste
- Cooking spray

Cooking Instructions:

1. Select BAKE, set the temperature to 375°F (191°C), and set the time to 25 minutes. Select START/STOP to start preheating.

2. Spray a casserole dish with cooking spray. In a medium bowl, beat the eggs, heavy cream, salt and pepper. Give the ingredients a good stir until creamy.

3. Stir in the breakfast sausage and Cheddar cheese. Pour the sausage mixture into the prepared casserole dish.

4. Place the dish directly in the pot. Close the hood and BAKE for 25 minutes, or until the top of the quiche is browned and the eggs are set.

5. Remove from the grill and allow to cool for a couple of minutes before serving. Serve and enjoy!

Pumpkin Egg Bake

Preparation time: 15 minutes

Cook time: 10 minutes

Total time: 25 minutes

Serves: 2

Ingredients:

- 2 eggs, beaten
- 1 tsp. cinnamon powder
- 1 tsp. baking soda
- 1 tbsp. olive oil
- ½ cup milk
- 2 cups flour
- 2 tbsp. cider vinegar
- 2 tsp. baking powder
- 1 tbsp. sugar
- 1 cup pumpkin purée

Cooking Instructions:

1. Select BAKE, set the temperature to 300°F (149°C), and set the time to 10 minutes. Select START/STOP to start preheating.

2. In a medium bowl, beat the eggs and add the milk, flour, cider vinegar, baking powder, sugar, pumpkin purée, cinnamon powder, and baking soda.

3. Give everything a good mix. Grease a baking pan with oil. Add the mixture to the pan. Place the pan directly in the pot.

4. Close the hood and BAKE for 10 minutes.

5. Serve hot and enjoy!

Spinach with Scrambled Eggs

Preparation time: 15 minutes

Cook time: 10 minutes

Total time: 25 minutes

Serves: 2

Ingredients:

- 5 oz. fresh spinach, chopped
- 1 large tomato, chopped
- 1 tsp. fresh lemon juice
- 2 tbsp. olive oil
- 4 eggs, whisked
- ½ tsp. coarse salt
- ½ tsp. ground black pepper
- ½ cup of fresh basil, chopped

Cooking Instructions:

1. Grease a baking pan with the oil. Select BAKE, set the temperature to 280°F (138°C), and set the time to 10 minutes.

2. Select START/STOP to start preheating. Add together the remaining ingredients in the greased pan, except the basil leaves.

3. Whisking the ingredients until combined. Place the pan directly in the pot. Close the hood and BAKE for 10 minutes.

4. Top with fresh basil leaves before serving.

5. Serve and enjoy!

BEEF & PORK RECIPES
Beef Schnitzel

Preparation time: 10 minutes

Cook time: 12 minutes

Total time: 22 minutes

Serves: 1

Ingredients:

- ½ cup friendly bread crumbs
- 1 thin beef schnitzel
- 2 tbsp. olive oil
- Pepper, to taste
- Salt, to taste
- 1 egg, beaten

Cooking Instructions:

1. Place the Crisper Basket and seal the hood. Press the AIR CRISP function, set the temperature to 350°F and set the time to 12 minutes.

2. Click the START/ STOP to start preheating. In a medium bowl, combine together the bread crumbs, oil, pepper, and salt.

3. In another bowl, add the beaten egg. Dredge the schnitzel in the egg before rolling it in the bread crumbs. Add the coated schnitzel in the Crisper Basket.

4. Close the hood and AIR CRISP for 12 minutes. Turn the schnitzel midway through the cooking.

5. Serve and enjoy!

Grilled Flank Steak

Preparation time: 15 minutes

Cook time: 8 minutes

Total time: 23 minutes

Serves: 2

Ingredients:

- ¼ tsp. freshly ground black pepper
- 2 (8-oz. / 227-g) flank steaks
- 1 tbsp. chili powder
- 1 tsp. dried oregano
- 2 tsp. ground cumin
- 1 tsp. sea salt

Cooking Instructions:

1. Insert the Grill Grate and seal the hood. Press the GRILL, set the temperature to HIGH, and set the time to 8 minutes.

2. Click the START/ STOP key to start preheating. Add together the chili powder, oregano, cumin, salt, and pepper in a medium bowl.

3. Rub the spice mixture with your hands on all sides of the steaks. Once the unit beeps, add the steaks on the Grill Grate.

4. Slowly press the steaks down to maximize grill marks. Close the hood and GRILL for 4 minutes. After 4 minutes, turn the steaks and seal the hood.

5. GRILL for additional 4 minutes. Open the hood and place the steaks on a cutting board. Allow to cool for a couple of minutes before slicing.

6. Serve and enjoy!

Baby Back Ribs

Preparation time: 15 minutes

Cook time: 22 minutes

Total time: 37 minutes

Serves: 4

Ingredients:

- 6 garlic cloves, minced
- 1 ½ tbsp. brown sugar
- 1 tbsp. grated fresh ginger
- 1 tsp. salt
- 4 (8- to 10-oz.) baby back ribs
- ¼ cup gochujang paste
- ¼ cup soy sauce
- ¼ cup freshly squeezed orange juice
- 2 tbsp. apple cider vinegar
- 2 tbsp. sesame oil

Cooking Instructions:

1. Add together the gochujang paste, soy sauce, orange juice, vinegar, oil, garlic, sugar, ginger, and salt in a medium bowl.

2. Give everything a good stir to combine. Transfer baby back ribs on a baking sheet and coat all sides with the sauce.

3. Cover with a piece of aluminum foil and refrigerate for at least 6 hours. Insert the Grill Grate and close the hood.

4. Press the GRILL function, set the temperature to MEDIUM, and set the time to 22 minutes. Press the START/ STOP function to start preheating.

5. Once the unit beeps, add the ribs on the Grill Grate. Close the hood and GRILL for 11 minutes. When the cooking cycle is complete, flip the ribs.

6. Close the hood, and GRILL for more 11 minutes. When cooking is complete, serve hot and enjoy!

Lamb Chops with Rosemary

Preparation time: 10 minutes

Cook time: 14 minutes

Total time: 24 minutes

Serves: 2

Ingredients:

- ½ rack lamb (4 bones)
- 3 tbsp. extra-virgin olive oil
- 1 garlic clove, minced
- 1 tbsp. fresh rosemary, chopped
- Sea salt, to taste
- Freshly ground black pepper, to taste

Cooking Instructions:

1. In a medium bowl, add together the oil, garlic, and rosemary. Give everything a good mix. Add the lamb in the bowl, using tongs to turn and coat with the oil.

2. Season the rack of lamb with the salt and pepper. Cover the lamb with a piece aluminum and refrigerate for at least 2 hours.

3. Insert the Grill Grate and close the hood. Press GRILL, set the temperature to HIGH, and set the time to 14 minutes.

4. Click START/ STOP to start preheating. Once the unit beeps, add the lamb on the Grill Grate. Close the hood and GRILL for 6 minutes.

5. After 6 minutes, turn the lamb and grill for additional 6 minutes. Check for doneness when the internal temperature of the lamb reaches 145°F (63°C) on a food thermometer.

6. If desired, GRILL for additional 2 minutes.

7. Serve and enjoy!

Korean BBQ Beef

Preparation time: 10 minutes

Cook time: 5 minutes

Total time: 15 minutes

Serves: 4

Ingredients:

- 1 lb. (454 g) rib eye steak, thinly sliced
- 2 scallions, thinly sliced, for garnish
- 1/3 cup soy sauce
- 2 tbsp. sesame oil
- 2 ½ tbsp. brown sugar
- 3 garlic cloves, minced
- ½ tsp. freshly ground black pepper
- Toasted sesame seeds, for garnish

Cooking Instructions:

1. Whisk together the soy sauce, sesame oil, brown sugar, garlic, and black pepper in a medium. Ensure that everything is well combined.

2. Add the beef into a large bowl and pour the sauce over the slices. Cover with a piece of aluminum foil and refrigerate for at least 1 hour.

3. Insert the Grill Grate and close the hood. Click GRILL, set the temperature to MEDIUM, and set the time to 5 minutes.

4. Press START/ STOP to begin preheating. Once the unit beeps, add the beef onto the Grill Grate. Close the hood and GRILL for 4 minutes without flipping.

5. After 4 minutes, check the steak for desired doneness. Grill for additional 1 minute if desired. When cooking is complete, transfer on to a serving bowl.

6. Top with scallions and sesame seeds and serve immediately.

Teriyaki Pork Ribs

Preparation time: 10 minutes

Cook time: 30 minutes

Total time: 40 minutes

Serves: 4

Ingredients:

- 4 (8-oz.) boneless country-style pork ribs
- ¼ cup soy sauce
- ¼ cup honey
- 1 tsp. garlic powder
- 1 tsp. ground dried ginger
- Cooking spray

Cooking Instructions:

1. Spray the Crisper Basket with cooking spray. Place the Crisper Basket and close the hood. Select AIR CRISP, set the temperature to 350°F (177°C).

2. Set the time to 30 minutes. Select START/ STOP to begin preheating. In a medium bowl, combine together the soy sauce, honey, garlic powder, and ginger.

3. Give everything a good stir to combine. Brush the ribs with half of the teriyaki sauce, then arrange the ribs in the basket.

4. Spritz with cooking spray. Work in batches to avoid overcrowding the Crisper Basket. Close the hood and AIR CRISP for 30 minutes.

5. Check for doneness when the internal temperature of the ribs reaches at least 145°F (63°C). Brush the ribs with remaining teriyaki sauce.

6. Turn the ribs midway through the cooking.

7. Serve and enjoy!

Beef Meatballs

Preparation time: 10 minutes

Cook time: 18 minutes

Total time: 28 minutes

Serves: 6

Ingredients:

- 1 lb. ground beef
- 1 tbsp. minced garlic
- ½ cup Mozzarella cheese
- 1 tsp. freshly ground pepper
- ½ cup grated Parmesan cheese

Cooking Instructions:

1. Insert the Crisper Basket and close the hood. Select AIR CRISP, set the temperature to 400°F (204°C), and set the time to 18 minutes.

2. Click START/ STOP to start preheating. Add all the ingredients in a medium bowl. Roll the meat mixture into 5 meatballs.

3. Once the unit beeps, place the meatballs to the Crisper Basket. Close the hood and AIR CRISP for 18 minutes.

4. Serve and enjoy!

Pork Tenderloin

Preparation time: 10 minutes

Cook time: 16 to 20 minutes

Total time: 30 minutes

Serves: 4

Ingredients:

- 1 (1 ½ lb.) pork tenderloin
- 2 tbsp. honey
- 1 tbsp. soy sauce
- ½ tsp. garlic powder
- ½ tsp. sea salt

Cooking Instructions:

1. Insert the Grill Grate and close the hood. Select GRILL, set the temperature to MEDIUM, and set the time to 20 minutes.

2. Click START/ STOP to start preheating. Add together the honey, soy sauce, garlic powder, and salt in a medium bowl. Give everything a good mix.

3. Once the unit beeps, add the pork tenderloin on the Grill Grate. Sprinkle all sides with the honey glaze. Close the hood and GRILL for 8 minutes.

4. After 8 minutes, turn the pork tenderloin and drizzle with any remaining glaze. Close the hood and GRILL for additional 7 minutes.

5. Check for doneness when the internal temperature of the pork reaches 145°F (63°C) on a food thermometer.

6. If desired, GRILL for additional 5 minutes. Transfer the pork on to a cutting board to rest for 5 minutes.

7. Slice and serve.

Lamb Ribs

Preparation time: 10 minutes

Cook time: 18 minutes

Total time: 28 minutes

Serves: 4

Ingredients:

- 2 tbsp. mustard
- 1 lb. lamb ribs
- ¼ cup mint leaves, chopped
- 1 cup Greek yogurt
- 1 tsp. rosemary, chopped
- Salt, to taste
- Freshly ground black pepper, to taste

Cooking Instructions:

1. Insert the Crisper Basket and close the hood. Select AIR CRISP, set the temperature to 350°F (177°C), and set the time to 18 minutes.

2. Click START/ STOP to start preheating. Rub the lamb ribs with the mustard and season with rosemary, salt, and pepper.

3. Once the unit beeps, add to the Crisper Basket. Close the hood and AIR CRISP for 18 minutes. In a medium bowl, combine the mint leaves and yogurt.

4. Add the lamb ribs to a serving bowl.

5. Serve with the mint yogurt and enjoy!

Korean-Style Steak Tips

Preparation time: 10 minutes

Cook time: 13 minutes

Total time: 23 minutes

Serves: 4

Ingredients:

- 4 garlic cloves, minced
- 1 ½ lb. beef tips
- ½ apple, peeled and grated
- 3 tbsp. sesame oil
- 3 tbsp. brown sugar
- 1/3 cup soy sauce
- 1 tsp. freshly ground black pepper
- Sea salt, to taste

Cooking Instructions:

1. Add together the garlic, apple, sesame oil, sugar, soy sauce, pepper, and salt in a medium bowl. Give everything a good mix to combine.

2. Add the beef tips in a bowl and pour the marinade over them. Cover with a piece of aluminum foil and refrigerate for at least 30 minutes.

3. Insert the Grill Grate and close the hood. Select GRILL, set the temperature to MEDIUM, and set the time to 13 minutes.

4. Click START/ STOP to start preheating. Once the unit beeps, add the steak tips on the Grill Grate. Close the hood and GRILL for 11 minutes.

5. Check for doneness when the internal temperature of the meat reaches 145°F (63°C) on a food thermometer.

6. If needed, GRILL for additional 2 minutes. Transfer the steak on to a cutting board to rest for 5 minutes.

7. Slice and serve.

POULTRY RECIPES
Mayonnaise-Mustard Chicken

Preparation time: 15 minutes

Cook time: 15 minutes

Total time: 30 minutes

Serves: 4

Ingredients:

- 1 lb. chicken tenders
- 6 tbsp. mayonnaise
- 2 tbsp. coarse-ground mustard
- 2 tsp. honey (optional)
- 2 tsp. curry powder
- 1 tsp. kosher salt
- 1 tsp. cayenne pepper

Cooking Instructions:

1. Insert the Crisper Basket and close the hood. Select BAKE, set the temperature to 350°F (177°C), and set the time to 15 minutes.

2. Click START/STOP to start preheating. Add together the mayonnaise, mustard, honey (if using), curry powder, salt, and cayenne in a medium bowl.

3. Add half of the mixture to a serving bowl and set aside. Add the chicken tenders to the large bowl and toss until well coated.

4. Transfer the tenders to the Crisper Basket. Close the hood and BAKE for 15 minutes.

5. Use a meat thermometer to ensure the chicken has reached an internal temperature of 165°F (74°C).

6. Serve the chicken with the dipping sauce.

Roasted Cajun Turkey

Preparation time: 15 minutes

Cook time: 30 minutes

Total time: 45 minutes

Serves: 4

Ingredients:

- 2 lb. turkey thighs, skinless and boneless
- 1 red onion, sliced
- 1 tbsp. Cajun seasoning mix
- 1 tbsp. fish sauce
- 2 cups chicken broth
- 2 bell peppers, sliced
- 1 habanero pepper, minced
- 1 carrot, sliced
- Nonstick cooking spray

Cooking Instructions:

1. Select ROAST, set the temperature to 360°F (182°C), and set the time to 30 minutes. Click START/STOP to start preheating.

2. Spray the bottom of the pot with nonstick cooking spray. Once the unit beeps, add the turkey thighs in the pot. Add the onion, peppers, and carrot.

3. Sprinkle with Cajun seasoning. Add the fish sauce and chicken broth. Close the hood and ROAST for 30 minutes until cooked through.

4. Serve warm and enjoy!

Lime Chicken with Cilantro

Preparation time: 25 minutes
Cook time: 20 minutes
Total time: 45 minutes
Serves: 4

Ingredients:
- 4 (4-oz.) boneless, skinless chicken breasts
- ½ cup chopped fresh cilantro
- Juice of 1 lime
- Chicken seasoning or rub, to taste
- Salt, to taste
- Freshly ground black pepper, to taste
- Cooking spray

Cooking Instructions:
1. In a medium bowl, add together the chicken breasts, cilantro, lime juice, chicken seasoning, salt, and black pepper. Toss to coat well.

2. Cover the bowl with piece of aluminum foil and refrigerate for at least 30 minutes. Spray the Crisper Basket with cooking spray.

3. Insert the Crisper Basket and close the hood. Select AIR CRISP, set the temperature to 400°F (204°C), and set the time to 10 minutes.

4. Select START/STOP to start preheating. Transfer the marinated chicken breasts to the grill. Spray with cooking spray.

5. Work in batches to avoid overcrowding the basket. Close the hood and AIR CRISP for 10 minutes or until the internal temperature of the chicken reaches at least 165°F (74°C).

6. Turn the chicken breast midway through the cooking. Serve immediately.

Cajun Turkey

Preparation time: 20 minutes

Cook time: 30 minutes

Total time: 50 minutes

Serves: 4

Ingredients:

- Roasted Cajun Turkey
- 2 lb. turkey thighs, skinless and boneless
- 1 tbsp. Cajun seasoning mix
- 1 tbsp. fish sauce
- 2 cups chicken broth
- 1 red onion, sliced
- 2 bell peppers, sliced
- 1 habanero pepper, minced
- 1 carrot, sliced
- Nonstick cooking spray

Cooking Instructions:

1. Select ROAST, set the temperature to 360°F (182°C), and set the time to 30 minutes. Select START/STOP to begin preheating.

2. Spritz the bottom and sides of the pot with nonstick cooking spray. Arrange the turkey thighs in the pot. Add the onion, peppers, and carrot.

3. Sprinkle with Cajun seasoning. Add the fish sauce and chicken broth. Close the hood and ROAST for 30 minutes until cooked through.

4. Serve hot and enjoy!

Chicken Breast

Preparation time: 15 minutes

Cook time: 20 minutes

Total time: 35 minutes

Serves: 4

Ingredients:
- 1 large egg, beaten
- ¾ cup Blackened seasoning
- 2 whole boneless, skinless chicken breasts (about 1 lb.), halved
- Cooking spray

Cooking Instructions:

1. Arrange a parchment paper on the Crisper Basket. Insert the Crisper Basket and close the hood.

2. Select AIR CRISP, set the temperature to 360°F (182°C), and set the time to 20 minutes. Select START/STOP to start preheating.

3. Add the beaten egg in one shallow bowl and the Blackened seasoning in a separate bowl. One at a time, dredge the chicken pieces in the beaten egg and the Blackened seasoning, coating thoroughly.

4. Place the chicken pieces on the parchment and spritz with cooking spray. Close the hood and AIR CRISP for 10 minutes.

5. Turn the chicken, drizzle with cooking spray. AIR CRISP for additional 10 minutes until the internal temperature reaches 165°F (74°C).

6. Allow it rest for a couple of minutes before serving.

Asian Turkey Meatballs

Preparation time: 15 minutes

Cook time: 11 to 14 minutes

Total time: 30 minutes

Serves: 4

Ingredients:

- 1 lb. ground turkey
- 2 tbsp. peanut oil, divided
- 1 medium onion, minced
- ¼ cup water chestnuts, chopped
- ½ tsp. ground ginger
- 2 tbsp. low-sodium soy sauce
- ¼ cup panko bread crumbs
- 1 egg, beaten

Cooking Instructions:

1. Select AIR CRISP, set the temperature to 400°F (204°C), and set the time to 2 minutes. Select START/STOP to begin preheating.

2. Add 1 tbsp. of peanut oil and onion in a round metal pan. Place the pan directly in the pot and close the hood.

3. Select AIR CRISP for 1 to 2 minutes or until crisp and tender. Transfer the onion to a medium bowl.

4. Add the water chestnuts, ground ginger, soy sauce, and bread crumbs to the onion and give everything a good mix.

5. Add egg and stir well. Mix in the ground turkey until combined. Form the mixture into 1-inch meatballs.

6. Drizzle the remaining 1 tablespoon of oil over the meatballs. Arrange the meatballs in the pan. Place the pan directly in the pot.

7. Close the hood and BAKE for 10 to 12 minutes, or until they are 165°F (74°C) on a meat thermometer.

8. Allow to sit for a couple of minutes before serving.

Spicy BBQ Chicken Drumsticks

Preparation time: 15 minutes

Cook time: 20 minutes

Total time: 35 minutes

Serves: 4

Ingredients:

- 1 lb. chicken drumsticks
- 2 cups barbecue sauce
- Juice of 1 lime
- 2 tbsp. honey
- 1 tbsp. hot sauce
- Sea salt, to taste
- Freshly ground black pepper, to taste

Cooking Instructions:

1. Add together the barbecue sauce, lime juice, honey, and hot sauce in a medium bowl. Season with salt and pepper.

2. Set aside ½ cup of the sauce. Add the drumsticks to the bowl and give everything a good mix. Insert the Grill Grate and close the hood.

3. Select GRILL, set the temperature to MEDIUM, and set the time to 20 minutes. Select START/STOP to start preheating.

4. Once the unit beeps, add the drumsticks on the Grill Grate. Close the hood and GRILL for 18 minutes.

5. Check for doneness once the internal temperature of the meat reaches at least 165°F (74°C) on a food thermometer.

6. If desired, close the hood and grill for additional 2 minutes. Serve and enjoy!

Turkey Meatloaves

Preparation time: 10 minutes

Cook time: 20

Total time: 30 minutes

Serves 4

Ingredients:

- ⅓ cup minced onion
- ¼ cup grated carrot
- 2 garlic cloves, minced
- 2 tbsp. ground almonds
- 2 tsp. olive oil
- 1 tsp. dried marjoram
- 1 egg white
- ¾ lb. ground turkey breast

Cooking Instructions:

1. Select BAKE, set the temperature to 400°F (204°C), and set the time to 24 minutes. Click START/STOP to start preheating.

2. Add together the onion, carrot, garlic, almonds, olive oil, marjoram, and egg white in a medium bowl. Give everything a good mix.

3. Add the ground turkey. Slowly mix the ingredients with the turkey until combined. Double 16 foil muffin cup liners to make 8 cups.

4. Divide the turkey mixture evenly among the liners. Transfer to the pot and close the hood. Bake for 20 to 24 minutes.

5. Check for doneness once the meatloaves reach an internal temperature of 165°F (74°C) on a meat thermometer.

6. Serve immediately and enjoy!

Turkey Tenderloin

Preparation time: 10 minutes

Cook time: 30 minutes

Total time: 40 minutes

Serves 4

Ingredients:

- 1½ lb. turkey breast tenderloin
- ½ tsp. paprika
- ½ tsp. freshly ground black pepper
- ½ tsp. garlic powder
- ½ tsp. salt
- Pinch cayenne pepper
- Olive oil spray

Cooking Instructions:

1. Spray the Crisper Basket with olive oil spray. Insert the Crisper Basket and close the hood.

2. Select AIR CRISP, set the temperature to 370°F (188°C), and set the time to 30 minutes. Select START/STOP to start preheating.

3. Add together the paprika, garlic powder, salt, black pepper, and cayenne pepper in a medium bowl. Coat the turkey with the mixture.

4. Add the turkey in the Crisper Basket. Spray the Crisper Basket with olive oil spray. Close the hood and AIR CRISP for 15 minutes.

5. Turn the turkey midway through the cooking and spray with olive oil spray. AIR CRISP until the internal temperature reaches at least 170°F (77°C) for more 10 to 15 minutes.

6. Let the turkey rest for 10 minutes before slicing and serving.

Teriyaki Chicken Wings

Preparation time: 15 minutes

Cook time: 14 minutes

Total time: 29

Serves: 4

Ingredients:

- 2 lb. bone-in chicken wings (drumettes and flats)
- 1 cup maple syrup
- ⅓ cup soy sauce
- ¼ cup teriyaki sauce
- 3 garlic cloves, minced
- 2 tsp. garlic powder
- 2 tsp. onion powder
- 1 tsp. freshly ground black pepper

Cooking Instructions:

1. Insert the Grill Grate and close the hood. Select GRILL, set the temperature to MEDIUM, and set the time to 14 minutes.

2. Click START/STOP to start preheating. Add together the maple syrup, soy sauce, teriyaki sauce, garlic, garlic powder, onion powder, and black pepper in a bowl.

3. Give everything a good whisk. Add the wings and toss to coat with the mixture. Once the unit beeps, add the chicken wings on the Grill Grate.

4. Close the hood and GRILL for 5 minutes. After 5 minutes, turn the wings, close the hood, and GRILL for more 5 minutes.

5. Check the wings for doneness when the internal temperature of the meat reaches at least 165°F (74°C) on a food thermometer.

6. If desired, GRILL for additional 4 minutes. Remove from the grill and serve.

Turkey Bell Peppers

Preparation time: 10 minutes

Cook time: 15 minutes

Total time: 35 minutes

Serves: 4

Ingredients:

- ½ lb. lean ground turkey
- 4 medium bell peppers
- 1 (15-oz.) can black beans, drained and rinsed
- 1 tsp. salt
- ½ tsp. ground cumin
- ½ tsp. freshly ground black pepper
- 1 cup shredded reduced-fat Cheddar cheese
- 1 cup cooked long-grain brown rice
- 1 cup mild salsa
- 1¼ tsp. chili powder
- Olive oil spray
- Chopped fresh cilantro, for garnish

Cooking Instructions:

1. Insert the Crisper Basket and close the hood. Select AIR CRISP, set the temperature to 360°F (182°C), and set the time to 15 minutes.

2. Click START/STOP to start preheating. In a large skillet over medium-high heat, sauté the turkey until browned, about 5 minutes.

3. Remove any excess fat. Cut about ½ inch off the tops of the peppers and then cut in half lengthwise. Remove and discard the seeds and set the peppers aside.

4. Add together the browned turkey, black beans, Cheddar cheese, rice, salsa, chili powder, salt, cumin, and black pepper in a large bowl.

5. Spoon the mixture into the bell peppers. Spritz the Crisper Basket with olive oil spray. Add the stuffed peppers in the Crisper Basket.

6. Close the hood and AIR CRISP for 10 to 15 minutes until heated through. Transfer to a serving bowl. Garnish with cilantro and serve.

Sweet and Sour Turkey Meatballs

Preparation time: 10 minutes

Cook time: 15 minutes

Total time: 25 minutes

Serves: 6

Ingredients:

- 1 lb. lean ground turkey
- ½ cup whole-wheat panko bread crumbs
- 1 egg, beaten
- 1 tbsp. soy sauce
- ¼ cup plus 1 tbsp. hoisin sauce, divided
- 2 tsp. minced garlic
- ⅛ tsp. salt
- ⅛ tsp. freshly ground black pepper
- 1 tsp. sriracha
- Olive oil spray

Cooking Instructions:

1. Spray the Crisper Basket with olive oil spray. Insert the Crisper Basket and close the hood.

2. Press AIR CRISP, set the temperature to 350°F (177°C), and set the time to 15 minutes. Click START/STOP to start preheating.

3. Add together the turkey, panko bread crumbs, egg, soy sauce, 1 tbsp. of hoisin sauce, garlic, salt, and black pepper in a medium bowl.

4. Form the mixture into 24 meatballs. In a medium bowl, combine the remaining ¼ cup of hoisin sauce and sriracha to make a glaze and set aside.

5. Add the meatballs in the Crisper Basket in a single layer. Close the hood and AIR CRISP for 8 minutes.

6. Rub the meatballs with the glaze and AIR CRISP until cooked through, for more 4 to 7 minutes.

7. Serve hot and enjoy!

Chicken Thighs

Preparation time: 15 minutes

Cook time: 10 minutes

Total time: 25 minutes

Serves: 4

Ingredients:

- 1 lb. boneless, skinless chicken thighs, cut crosswise into thirds
- ¼ cup chopped fresh cilantro, for garnish
- ¼ cup julienned peeled fresh ginger
- 2 tbsp. vegetable oil
- 1 tbsp. honey
- 1 tbsp. soy sauce
- 1 tbsp. ketchup
- 1 tsp. garam masala
- 1 tsp. ground turmeric
- ¼ tsp. kosher salt
- ½ tsp. cayenne pepper
- Vegetable oil spray

Cooking Instructions:

1. Add together the ginger, oil, honey, soy sauce, ketchup, garam masala, turmeric, salt, and cayenne in a medium bowl. Whisk until well combined.

2. Add the chicken in a resealable plastic bag and pour the marinade over. Seal the bag and shake to coat both sides chicken with the marinade.

3. Refrigerator for at least 24 hours. Insert the Crisper Basket and close the hood. Select BAKE, set the temperature to 350°F (177°C), and set the time to 10 minutes.

4. Select START/STOP to start preheating. Spray the Crisper Basket with vegetable oil spray and add the chicken.

5. Close the hood and BAKE for 10 minutes. Check for doneness when the internal temperature pf the chicken reaches 165°F (74°C).

6. Transfer the chicken to a serving bowl.

7. Garnish with cilantro and serve.

VEGAN & VEGETARIAN
Roasted Garlic and Asparagus

Preparation time: 10 minutes

Cook time: 10 minutes

Total time: 20 minutes

Serves: 4

Ingredients:

- 1 lb. asparagus, woody ends trimmed
- 2 tbsp. olive oil
- 1 tbsp. balsamic vinegar
- 2 tsp. minced garlic
- Salt, to taste
- Freshly ground black pepper, to taste

Cooking Instructions:

1. Insert the Crisper Basket and close the hood. Select ROAST, set the temperature to 400°F (204°C), and set the time to 10 minutes.

2. Click START/STOP to start preheating. Add together the asparagus with the olive oil, balsamic vinegar, garlic, salt, and pepper in a medium bowl.

3. Toss everything until thoroughly coated. Place the asparagus in the Crisper Basket. Close the hood and ROAST for 10 minutes until crispy.

4. Turn the asparagus midway through the cooking.

5. Serve hot and enjoy!

Cheese Stuffed Vegetable

Preparation time: 15 minutes

Cook time: 16 to 20 minutes

Total time: 30 minutes

Serves: 4

Ingredients:

- 4 medium beefsteak tomatoes, rinsed
- ½ cup grated carrot
- 1 small onion, chopped
- 1 garlic clove, minced
- 2 tsp. olive oil
- 2 cups fresh baby spinach
- ¼ cup crumbled low-sodium feta cheese
- ½ tsp. dried basil

Cooking Instructions:

1. Select BAKE, set the temperature to 350°F (177°C), and set the time to 20 minutes. Select START/STOP to start preheating.

2. Cut the top of each tomato on your cutting board and scoop out a ¼- to ½-inch-thick tomato pulp. Add the tomatoes upside down on paper towels to drain.

3. Add the carrot, onion, garlic, and olive oil in a baking pan and stir. Place the pan directly in the pot.

4. Close the hood and BAKE for 4 to 6 minutes or until tender. Remove the pan from the grill and stir in the spinach, feta cheese, and basil.

5. Spoon ¼ of the vegetable mixture into each tomato and add the stuffed tomatoes to the pan. Place the pan directly in the pot.

6. Close the hood and BAKE for 12 to 14 minutes, or until the tomatoes are caramelized. Allow the tomatoes cool for a couple of minutes.

7. Serve and enjoy!

Kidney Beans Oatmeal

Preparation time: 10 minutes

Cook time: 6 minutes

Total time: 16 minutes

Serves: 2 to 4

Ingredients:

- 2 medium bell peppers, halved lengthwise, deseeded
- ½ tsp. paprika
- ½ tsp. salt
- ¼ tsp. black pepper powder
- 2 tbsp. cooked kidney beans
- 2 tbsp. cooked chick peas
- 2 cups cooked oatmeal
- 1 tsp. ground cumin
- ¼ cup yogurt

Cooking Instructions:

1. Insert the Crisper Basket and close the hood. Select AIR CRISP, set the temperature to 355°F (179°C), and set the time to 6 minutes.

2. Click START/STOP to start preheating. Add the bell peppers, cut-side down, in the Crisper Basket. Close the hood and AIR CRISP for 2 minutes.

3. Transfer the peppers to a bowl and allow to cool for a couple of minutes. In a medium bowl, combine the remaining ingredients.

4. Divide the mixture evenly and use each portion to stuff a pepper. Place the stuffed peppers to the basket. Close the hood and AIR CRISP for 4 minutes.

5. Serve warm and enjoy!

Brussel Sprouts

Preparation time: 10 minutes

Cook time: 15 minutes

Total time: 25 minutes

Serves: 4

Ingredients:

- 1 lb. Brussels sprouts, halved
- 1 cup bread crumbs
- 2 tbsp. grated Grana Padano cheese
- 1 tbsp. paprika
- 2 tbsp. canola oil
- 1 tbsp. chopped sage

Cooking Instructions:

1. Arrange a parchment paper into the Crisper Basket. Insert the Crisper Basket and close the hood.

2. Select ROAST, set the temperature to 400°F (204°C), and set the time to 15 minutes. Select START/STOP to start preheating.

3. Add together the bread crumbs, cheese, and paprika in a medium bowl. In a large bowl, add the Brussels sprouts and spray with canola oil.

4. Sprinkle with the bread crumb mixture and toss to coat. Add the Brussels sprouts in the Crisper Basket. Close the hood and ROAST for 15 minutes, or until crisp.

5. Shake the basket a few times halfway through the cooking. Transfer the Brussels sprouts to a plate and sprinkle the sage.

6. Serve and enjoy!

Rosemary Potatoes

Preparation time: 10 minutes

Cook time: 20 to 22 minutes

Total time: 30 minutes

Serves: 4

Ingredients:

- 1½ lb. medium red potatoes, cut into 1-inch cubes
- 2 tbsp. olive oil
- 2 tbsp. minced fresh rosemary
- 1 tbsp. minced garlic
- 1 tsp. salt, plus additional as needed
- ½ tsp. freshly ground black pepper

Cooking Instructions:

1. Insert the Crisper Basket and close the hood. Select ROAST, set the temperature to 400°F (204°C), and set the time to 22 minutes.

2. Click START/STOP to start preheating. In a medium bowl, combine together the potato cubes with the olive oil, rosemary, garlic, salt, and pepper.

3. Toss the ingredients until thoroughly coated. Arrange the potato cubes in the Crisper Basket in a single layer.

4. Close the hood and ROAST for 20 to 22 minutes until the potatoes are tender. Shake the basket a few times halfway through the cooking.

5. Transfer from the basket to a serving bowl. Taste and add additional salt and pepper as needed.

6. Serve and enjoy!

Italian Tofu

Preparation time: 10 minutes

Cook time: 10 minutes

Total time: 20 minutes

Serves: 2

Ingredients:

- 6 oz. extra firm tofu, pressed and cubed
- 1 tbsp. soy sauce
- 1 tbsp. water
- ⅓ tsp. garlic powder
- ⅓ tsp. onion powder
- ⅓ tsp. dried oregano
- ⅓ tsp. dried basil
- Black pepper, to taste

Cooking Instructions:

1. Add together the soy sauce, water, garlic powder, onion powder, oregano, basil, and black pepper in a medium bowl.

2. Whisk the ingredients until combined. Add the tofu cubes, stirring to coat, and let them marinate for 10 minutes.

3. Select BAKE, set the temperature to 390°F (199°C), and set the time to 10 minutes. Select START/STOP to start preheating.

4. Add the tofu in the baking pan. Place the pan directly in the pot. Close the hood and BAKE for 10 minutes until crisp.

5. Turn the tofu midway through the cooking. Transfer from the basket to a serving bowl.

6. Serve and enjoy!

Cabbage and Red Pepper Flakes

Preparation time: 10 minutes

Cook time: 7 minutes

Total time: 17 minutes

Serves: 4

Ingredients:

- 1 head cabbage, sliced into 1-inch-thick ribbons
- 1 tbsp. olive oil
- 1 tsp. garlic powder
- 1 tsp. red pepper flakes
- 1 tsp. salt
- 1 tsp. freshly ground black pepper

Cooking Instructions:

1. Insert the Crisper Basket and close the hood. Select ROAST, set the temperature to 350°F (177°C), and set the time to 7 minutes.

2. Press START/STOP to start preheating. In a medium bowl, add the cabbage with the olive oil, garlic powder, red pepper flakes, salt, and pepper.

3. Toss the ingredients until well coated. Arrange the cabbage in the Crisper Basket. Close the hood and ROAST for 7 minutes until crisp.

4. Turn the cabbage with tongs midway through the cooking. Transfer from the basket to a serving bowl.

5. Serve hot and enjoy!

Spicy Broccoli with Parmesan

Preparation time: 10 minutes

Cook time: 4 minutes

Total time: 14 minutes

Serves: 4

Ingredients:

- 1 lb. broccoli florets
- 1 medium shallot, minced
- 2 tbsp. olive oil
- 2 tbsp. unsalted butter, melted
- 2 tsp. minced garlic
- ¼ cup grated Parmesan cheese

Cooking Instructions:

1. Insert the Crisper Basket and close the hood. Select ROAST, set the temperature to 360°F (182°C), and set the time to 4 minutes.

2. Select START/STOP to start preheating. In a medium bowl, add together the broccoli florets with the shallot, olive oil, butter, garlic, and Parmesan cheese.

3. Toss the ingredients until the broccoli florets are thoroughly coated. Arrange the broccoli florets in the Crisper Basket in a single layer.

4. Close the hood and ROAST for 4 minutes until crisp-tender.

5. Serve hot and enjoy!

Acorn Squash

Preparation time: 10 minutes

Cook time: 15 minutes

Total time: 25 minutes

Serves: 2

Ingredients:

- 1 small acorn squash, halved and deseeded
- 1 tsp. coconut oil
- 1 tsp. light brown sugar
- Pinch of ground cinnamon
- Pinch of ground nutmeg

Cooking Instructions:

1. Insert the Crisper Basket and close the hood. Select AIR CRISP, set the temperature to 325°F (163°C), and set the time to 15 minutes.

2. Click START/STOP to start preheating. Transfer the acorn squash on a clean work surface and brush both sides with coconut oil.

3. Sprinkle with the brown sugar, cinnamon, and nutmeg. Add the squash halves in the Crisper Basket, cut-side up.

4. Close the hood and AIR CRISP for 15 minutes or until tender. Allow to rest for a couple of minutes.

5. Serve hot and enjoy!

Roasted Ratatouille

Preparation time: 10 minutes

Cook time: 16 minutes

Total time: 26 minutes

Serves: 2

Ingredients:

- Roma tomatoes, sliced
- 1 zucchini, sliced
- 2 tbsp. herbes de Provence
- 1 tbsp. vinegar
- 2 yellow bell peppers, sliced
- 2 garlic cloves, minced
- 2 tbsp. olive oil
- Salt, to taste
- Freshly ground black pepper, to taste

Cooking Instructions:

1. Select ROAST, set the temperature to 390°F (199°C), and set the time to 16 minutes. Select START/STOP to start preheating.

2. In a medium bowl, add together the tomatoes, zucchini, bell peppers, garlic, olive oil, herbes de Provence, and vinegar.

3. Toss the vegetables until they are evenly coated. Season with salt and pepper and toss again. Pour the vegetable mixture into the pot.

4. Close the hood and ROAST for 8 minutes. Stir and roast for about 8 minutes or until tender. Allow the vegetable mixture to rest for about 5 minutes.

5. Serve and enjoy!

BEEF & PORK RECIPES
Breaded Scallops

Preparation time: 10 minutes

Cook time: 6 to 8 minutes

Total time: 18 minutes

Serves: 4

Ingredients:

- 1 lb. fresh scallops
- 1 egg, beaten
- 3 tbsp. flour
- 1 cup of bread crumbs
- 2 tbsp. olive oil
- Salt, to taste
- Black pepper, to taste

Cooking Instructions:

1. Insert the Crisper Basket and close the hood. Select AIR CRISP, set the temperature to 360°F (182°C), and set the time to 8 minutes.

2. Select START/STOP to start preheating. Beat the egg in a bowl. Add the flour and bread crumbs into separate bowls.

3. Dip the scallops in the flour and remove any excess. Dip the flour-coated scallops in the beaten egg and roll in the bread crumbs.

4. Brush the scallops with olive oil and season with salt and pepper, to taste. Transfer the scallops in the Crisper Basket.

5. Close the hood and AIR CRISP for 6 to 8 minutes, or until the scallops reaches an internal temperature of 145°F (63°C) on a meat thermometer.

6. Shake the basket midway through the cooking. Allow the scallops to cool for a couple of minutes.

7. Serve and enjoy!

Beef Schnitzel

Preparation time: 10 minutes

Cook time: 12 minutes

Total time: 22 minutes

Serves: 1

Ingredients:

- 1 thin beef schnitzel
- ½ cup friendly bread crumbs
- 2 tbsp. olive oil
- Salt, to taste
- Pepper, to taste
- 1 egg, beaten

Cooking Instructions:

1. Insert the Crisper Basket and close the hood. Select AIR CRISP, set the temperature to 350°F (177°C), and set the time to 12 minutes.

2. Select START/STOP to start preheating. Add together the bread crumbs, oil, pepper, and salt in a medium bowl.

3. In another bowl, beaten the egg. Dip the schnitzel in the egg before rolling it in the bread crumbs. Add the coated schnitzel in the Crisper Basket.

4. Close the hood and AIR CRISP for 12 minutes. Turn the schnitzel midway through the cooking.

5. Serve and enjoy!

Lamb Ribs

Preparation time: 10 minutes

Cook time: 18 minutes

Total time: 28 minutes

Serves: 4

Ingredients:

- 1 lb. lamb ribs
- 1 tsp. rosemary, chopped
- 2 tbsp. mustard
- Salt, to taste
- Freshly ground black pepper, to taste
- ¼ cup mint leaves, chopped
- 1 cup Greek yogurt

Cooking Instructions:

1. Insert the Crisper Basket and close the hood. Select AIR CRISP, set the temperature to 350°F (177°C), and set the time to 18 minutes.

2. Click START/STOP to start preheating. Rub the mustard to the lamb ribs, and season with rosemary, salt, and pepper.

3. Transfer to the basket. Close the hood and AIR CRISP for 18 minutes. In a medium bowl, combine together the mint leaves and yogurt.

4. Transfer the lamb ribs from the grill to a serving bowl. Serve with the mint yogurt and enjoy!

Pork Chops

Preparation time: 10 minutes

Cook time: 35 minutes

Total time: 45 minutes

Serves: 4

Ingredients:

- 4 boneless pork chops
- 3 tbsp. Worcestershire sauce
- ½ tbsp. dry mustard powder
- 2 cups ketchup
- ¾ cup bourbon
- ¼ cup apple cider vinegar
- ¼ cup soy sauce
- 1 cup packed brown sugar
- Sea salt, to taste
- Freshly ground black pepper, to taste

Cooking Instructions:

1. Add together the ketchup, bourbon, vinegar, soy sauce, sugar, Worcestershire sauce, and mustard powder in a saucepan over medium high heat.

2. Give everything a good stir to combine and bring to a boil. Reduce the heat to low and simmer, uncovered and stirring occasionally, for 20 minutes.

3. Once thickened, remove the pan from the heat and set aside. While the barbecue sauce is cooking, insert the Grill Grate into the unit and close the hood.

4. Select GRILL, set the temperature to MEDIUM, and set the time to 15 minutes. Select START/STOP to start preheating.

5. Once the unit beeps, add the pork chops on the Grill Grate. Close the hood, and GRILL for 8 minutes.

6. After 8 minutes, turn the pork chops and sprinkle with the barbecue sauce. Close the hood, and GRILL for 5 minutes more.

7. Remove the hood and turn the pork chops again. Sprinkle both sides with the barbecue sauce and close the hood.

8. GRILL the pork chops for additional 2 minutes. When cooking is done, season with salt and pepper. Serve and enjoy!

Pork Tenderloin

Preparation time: 10 minutes

Cook time: 15 to 20 minutes

Total time: 30 minutes

Serves: 4

Ingredients:

- 1 (1½ lb.) pork tenderloin
- 2 tbsp. honey
- 1 tbsp. soy sauce
- ½ tsp. garlic powder
- ½ tsp. sea salt

Cooking Instructions:

1. Insert the Grill Grate and close the hood. Select GRILL, set the temperature to MEDIUM, and set the time to 20 minutes.

2. Click START/STOP to start preheating. In a medium bowl, add together the honey, soy sauce, garlic powder, and salt.

3. Once the unit beeps, add the pork tenderloin on the Grill Grate. Sprinkle both sides with the honey glaze.

4. Close the hood and GRILL for 8 minutes. After 8 minutes, turn the pork tenderloin and sprinkle with any remaining glaze.

5. Close the hood and GRILL for additional 7 minutes. Check for doneness when the internal temperature of the pork reaches 145°F (63°C) on a food thermometer.

6. If desired, GRILL for additional 5 minutes. Transfer the pork onto on a cutting board to rest for a couple of minutes.

7. Slice and serve.

Flank Steak

Preparation time: 15 minutes

Cook time: 8 minutes

Total: 23 minutes

Serves: 2

Ingredients:

- 2 (8-oz.) flank steaks
- 1 tbsp. chili powder
- 1 tsp. dried oregano
- 2 tsp. ground cumin
- 1 tsp. sea salt
- ¼ tsp. freshly ground black pepper

Cooking Instructions:

1. Insert the Grill Grate and close the hood. Select GRILL, set the temperature to HIGH, and set the time to 8 minutes.

2. Select START/STOP to start preheating. Add together chili powder, oregano, cumin, salt, and pepper in a medium bowl.

3. Rub the spice mixture on all sides of the steaks with your hands. Once the unit beeps, add the steaks on the Grill Grate.

4. Slowly place the steaks down to maximize grill marks. Close the hood and GRILL for 4 minutes. After 4 minutes, turn the steaks.

5. Close the hood, and GRILL for additional 4 minutes. Transfer the steaks from the grill to a cutting board.

6. Allow the steak rest for a couple of minutes before slicing.

7. Serve and enjoy!

Korean BBQ Beef

Preparation time: 10 minutes

Cook time: 5 minutes

Total time: 15 minutes

Serves 4

Ingredients:

- 1 lb. rib eye steak, thinly sliced
- 2 scallions, thinly sliced, for garnish
- ⅓ cup soy sauce
- 2 tbsp. sesame oil
- 2½ tbsp. brown sugar
- 3 garlic cloves, minced
- ½ tsp. freshly ground black pepper
- Toasted sesame seeds, for garnish

Cooking Instructions:

1. Add together the soy sauce, sesame oil, brown sugar, garlic, and black pepper in a medium bowl. Toss the ingredients until fully combined.

2. In a medium bowl, add the beef and pour the sauce over the slices. Cover with a piece of aluminum foil and refrigerate for at least 1 hour.

3. Insert the Grill Grate and close the hood. Select GRILL, set the temperature to MEDIUM, and set the time to 5 minutes.

4. Select START/STOP to start preheating. Once the unit beeps, add the beef onto the Grill Grate. Close the hood and GRILL for 4 minutes.

5. After 4 minutes, check the steak for desired doneness. Grill for additional 1 minute, if needed. When cooking is complete, top with scallions and sesame seeds.

6. Serve and enjoy!

Baby Back Ribs

Preparation time: 15 minutes

Cook time: 22 minutes

Total time: 37 minutes

Serves: 4

Ingredients:

- 4 (8- to 10-oz.) baby back ribs
- ¼ cup gochujang paste
- ¼ cup soy sauce
- ¼ cup freshly squeezed orange juice
- 2 tbsp. apple cider vinegar
- 2 tbsp. sesame oil
- 6 garlic cloves, minced
- 1½ tbsp brown sugar
- 1 tbsp. grated fresh ginger
- 1 tsp. salt

Cooking Ingredients:

1. Add together the gochujang paste, soy sauce, orange juice, vinegar, oil, garlic, sugar, ginger, and salt in a medium bowl.

2. Give everything a good stir to combine. Add the baby back ribs on a baking sheet and toss to coat with the sauce.

3. Cover and refrigerate for at least 6 hours. Insert the Grill Grate and close the hood. Select GRILL, set the temperature to MEDIUM, and set the time to 22 minutes.

4. Select START/STOP to start preheating. Once the unit beeps, add the ribs on the Grill Grate. Close the hood and GRILL for 11 minutes.

5. After 11 minutes, turn the ribs. Close the hood, and GRILL for another 11 minutes.

6. Serve and enjoy!

Lamb Chops with Rosemary

Preparation time: 15 minutes

Cook time: 14 minutes

Total time: 29 minutes

Serves: 2

Ingredients:

- ½ rack lamb (4 bones)
- 3 tbsp. extra-virgin olive oil
- 1 garlic clove, minced
- 1 tbsp. fresh rosemary, chopped
- Sea salt, to taste
- Freshly ground black pepper, to taste

Cooking Instructions:

1. In a medium bowl, add together the oil, garlic, and rosemary. Season the rack of lamb with the salt and pepper.

2. Add the lamb in the bowl and toss to coat with the oil mixture. Cover and refrigerate for 2 hours.

3. Insert the Grill Grate and close the hood. Select GRILL, set the temperature to HIGH, and set the time to 14 minutes.

4. Select START/STOP to start preheating. Once the unit beeps, add the lamb on the Grill Grate. Close the hood and GRILL for 6 minutes.

5. After 6 minutes, turn the lamb and grill for additional 6 minutes. Check for doneness when the internal temperature of the lamb reaches 145°F (63°C) on a food thermometer.

6. If desired, GRILL for additional 2 minutes.

7. Serve and enjoy!

Beef Meatballs

Preparation time: 10 minutes

Cook time: 18 minutes

Total time: 28 minutes

Serves: 6

Ingredients:

- 1 lb. ground beef
- ½ cup grated Parmesan cheese
- 1 tbsp. minced garlic
- ½ cup Mozzarella cheese
- 1 tsp. freshly ground pepper

Cooking Instructions:

1. Insert the Crisper Basket and close the hood. Select AIR CRISP, set the temperature to 400°F (204°C), and set the time to 18 minutes.

2. Select START/STOP to start preheating. Add together all of the ingredients in a bowl and mix thoroughly.

3. Roll the meat mixture into 5 meatballs. Place to Crisper Basket. Close the hood and AIR CRISP for 18 minutes.

4. Serve and enjoy!

Pork Meatballs

Preparation time: 10 minutes

Cook time: 15 minutes

Total time: 25 minutes

Serves: 4

Ingredients:

- 1 lb. ground pork
- 2 cloves garlic, finely minced
- 1 cup scallions, finely chopped
- 1½ tbsp. Worcestershire sauce
- ½ tsp. freshly grated ginger root
- 1 tsp. turmeric powder
- 1 tbsp. oyster sauce
- 1 medium sliced red chili, for garnish
- Cooking spray

Cooking Instructions:

1. Spray the Crisper Basket with cooking spray. Insert the Crisper Basket and close the hood. Select AIR CRISP, set the temperature to 350°F (177°C).

2. Set the time to 15 minutes. Select START/STOP to start preheating. In a medium bowl, add together all of the ingredients, except for the red chili.

3. Toss the ingredients to combine. Shape the mixture into equally sized balls and add into the Crisper Basket.

4. Spray with cooking spray. Close the hood and AIR CRISP for 15 minutes or until the balls are browned. Turn the balls midway through the cooking.

5. Serve with red chili on top and enjoy!

Teriyaki Pork Ribs

Preparation time: 10 minutes

Cook time: 30 minutes

Total time: 40 minutes

Serves: 4

Ingredients:

- 4 (8-oz.) boneless country-style pork ribs
- ¼ cup soy sauce
- ¼ cup honey
- 1 tsp. garlic powder
- 1 tsp. ground dried ginger
- Cooking spray

Cooking Instructions:

1. Spray the Crisper Basket with cooking spray. Insert the Crisper Basket and close the hood. Select AIR CRISP, set the temperature to 350°F (177°C).

2. Set the time to 30 minutes. Select START/STOP to start preheating. In a medium bowl, add together the soy sauce, honey, garlic powder, and ginger.

3. Give everything a good stir to make the teriyaki sauce. Brush the ribs with half of the teriyaki sauce and transfer the ribs to the Crisper Basket.

4. Spray with cooking spray. Close the hood and AIR CRISP for 30 minutes or until the internal temperature of the ribs reaches at least 145°F (63°C).

5. Brush the ribs with rest of the teriyaki sauce and turn midway through the cooking. Serve and enjoy!

Pork Sausage

Preparation time: 10 minutes

Cook time: 27 minutes

Total time: 37 minutes

Serves: 6

Ingredients:

- 6 pork sausages, chopped
- 1 lb. cauliflower, chopped
- ½ onion, sliced
- 3 eggs, beaten
- ⅓ cup Colby cheese
- 1 tsp. cumin powder
- ½ tsp. tarragon
- ½ tsp. sea salt
- ½ tsp. ground black pepper
- Cooking spray

Cooking Instructions:

1. Select BAKE, set the temperature to 365°F (185°C), and set the time to 27 minutes. Select START/STOP to start preheating.

2. Spray a baking pan with cooking spray. Add the cauliflower in a saucepan over medium heat and boil until tender.

3. In a food processor, add the boiled cauliflower and pulse until puréed. Transfer to a large bowl and add the remaining ingredients until well blended.

4. Add the cauliflower and sausage mixture into the baking pan. Place the pan directly in the pot. Close the hood and BAKE for 27 minutes, or until lightly browned.

5. Serve hot and enjoy!

Vietnamese Pork Chops

Preparation time: 10 minutes

Cook time: 12 minutes

Total time: 22 minutes

Serves: 2

Ingredients:

- 2 pork chops
- 1 tbsp. chopped shallot
- 1 tbsp. chopped garlic
- 1 tbsp. fish sauce
- 3 tbsp. lemongrass
- 1 tsp. soy sauce
- 1 tbsp. brown sugar
- 1 tbsp. olive oil
- 1 tsp. ground black pepper

Cooking Instructions:

1. In a medium bowl, add together the shallot, garlic, fish sauce, lemongrass, soy sauce, brown sugar, olive oil, and pepper.

2. Give everything a good stir to combine. Add the pork chops in the bowl and toss to coat. Transfer the bowl in the refrigerator to marinate for at least 2 hours.

3. Insert the Crisper Basket and close the hood. Select AIR CRISP, set the temperature to 400°F (204°C), and set the time to 12 minutes.

4. Select START/STOP to start preheating. Remove the pork chops from the bowl and discard the marinade. Add the chops into the Crisper Basket.

5. Close the hood and AIR CRISP for 12 minutes or until lightly browned. Turn the pork chops midway through the cooking time.

6. Remove the pork chops from the basket to a serving bowl. Serve warm and enjoy!

FISH & SEAFOOD RECIPES
Coconut Chili Fish Curry

Preparation time: 15 minutes

Cook time: 20 to 22 minutes

Total time: 35 minutes

Serves: 4

Ingredients:

- 1 lb. fish, chopped
- 1 ripe tomato, pureed
- 2 tbsp. sunflower oil, divided
- 2 red chilies, chopped
- 1 shallot, minced
- 1 garlic clove, minced
- 1 cup coconut milk
- 1 tbsp. coriander powder
- 1 tsp. red curry paste
- ½ tsp. fenugreek seeds
- Salt, to taste
- White pepper, to taste

Cooking Instructions:

1. Insert the Crisper Basket and close the hood. Select AIR CRISP, set the temperature to 380°F (193°C), and set the time to 10 minutes.

2. Click START/STOP to start preheating. Brush the Crisper Basket with 1 tablespoon of sunflower oil. Add the fish in the basket.

3. Close the hood and AIR CRISP for 10 minutes. Turn the fish midway through the cooking. Grease a baking pan with the remaining 1 tbsp. of sunflower oil.

4. Transfer the cooked fish to the baking pan. Stir in the rest of the ingredients and return to the grill.

5. Reduce the temperature to 350°F (177°C) and AIR CRISP for additional 10 to 12 minutes until heated through. Allow to cool for a couple of minutes before serving.

6. Serve and enjoy!

Paprika Shrimp

Preparation time: 10 minutes

Cook time: 10 minutes

Total time: 20 minutes

Serves: 4

Ingredients:

- 1 lb. tiger shrimp
- ¼ tbsp. smoked paprika
- ¼ tsp. cayenne pepper
- 2 tbsp. olive oil
- ½ tbsp. old bay seasoning
- Dash of sea salt

Cooking Instructions:

1. Insert the Crisper Basket and close the hood. Select AIR CRISP, set the temperature to 380°F (193°C), and set the time to 10 minutes.

2. Select START/STOP to start preheating. In a medium bowl, toss all the ingredients until the shrimp are evenly coated.

3. Place the shrimp in the Crisper Basket. Close the hood and AIR CRISP for 10 minutes, shaking the basket midway through the cooking.

4. Cook until the shrimp are no longer pink.

5. Serve warm and enjoy!

Shrimp Tacos

Preparation time: 15 minutes

Cook time: 10 to 15 minutes

Total time: 30 minutes

Serves: 4

Ingredients:

- 1 (14-oz.) bag coleslaw mix
- 2 limes, cut in half
- 12 oz. small shrimp, deveined, with tails off
- 1 tsp. olive oil
- 1 - 2 tap. Blackened seasoning
- 8 corn tortillas, warmed
- Cooking spray

Cooking Instructions:

1. Insert the Crisper Basket and close the hood. Select AIR CRISP, set the temperature to 400°F (204°C), and set the time to 15 minutes.

2. Click START/STOP to start preheating. Spritz the Crisper Basket with cooking spray. Pat the shrimp dry with a paper towel to absorb any excess water.

3. Add the shrimp with olive oil and Blackened seasoning in a medium bowl. Toss the ingredients to combine. Add the shrimp in the Crisper Basket.

4. Close the hood and AIR CRISP for 5 minutes. Shake the basket, lightly spray with cooking spray. Cook until the shrimp begins to brown for 5 to 10 more minutes.

5. Fill each tortilla with the coleslaw mix and top with the blackened shrimp. Squeeze fresh lime juice over top.

6. Serve and enjoy!

Crab Ratatouille

Preparation time: 10 minutes

Cook time: 11 to 14 minutes

Total time: 29 minutes

Serves: 4

Ingredients:

- 1½ cups cooked crab meat
- 1½ cups peeled and cubed eggplant
- 1 tbsp. olive oil
- ½ tsp. dried basil
- 2 large tomatoes, chopped
- 1 red bell pepper, chopped
- 1 onion, chopped
- ½ tsp. dried thyme
- Pinch salt
- Freshly ground black pepper, to taste

Cooking Instructions:

1. Select ROAST, set the temperature to 400°F (204°C)., and set the time to 15 minutes. Select START/STOP to start preheating.

2. Add together the eggplant, tomatoes, bell pepper, onion, olive oil, basil and thyme into the pot. Toss the ingredients to combine.

3. Season with salt and pepper. Close the hood and ROAST for 9 minutes. Add the crab meat and give everything a good stir.

4. Roast for additional 2 to 5 minutes, or until the vegetables are softened. Serve warm and enjoy!

Shrimp and Vegetable Paella

Preparation time: 10 minutes

Cook time: 14 to 17 minutes

Total time: 27 minutes

Serves: 4

Ingredients:

- 1 cup frozen cooked small shrimp
- ½ cup frozen baby peas
- 1 tomato, diced
- 1 (10-oz.) package frozen cooked rice, thawed
- 1 (6-oz.) jar artichoke hearts, drained and chopped
- ¼ cup vegetable broth
- ½ tsp. dried thyme
- ½ tsp. turmeric

Cooking Instructions:

1. Select BAKE, set the temperature to 340°F (171°C), and set the time to 17 minutes. Select START/STOP to start preheating.

2. In a baking pan, add together the cooked rice, chopped artichoke hearts, vegetable broth, thyme, and turmeric. Give everything a good stir to combine.

3. Place the pan directly in the pot. Close the hood and BAKE for 9 minutes, or until the rice is heated through.

4. Remove the pan from the grill and fold in the shrimp, baby peas, and diced tomato. Give everything a good mix.

5. Transfer to the grill and bake for 5 to 8 minutes, or until the shrimp are done and the paella is bubbling.

6. Allow to rest for a couple of minutes before serving.

7. Serve and enjoy!

Cod Fillet with Sesame Seeds

Preparation time: 10 minutes

Cook time: 7 to 9 minutes

Total time: 19 minutes

Serves: 1

Ingredients:

- 6 oz. (170 g) fresh cod fillet
- 1 tsp. sesame seeds
- 1 tbsp. reduced-sodium soy sauce
- 2 tsp. honey
- Cooking spray

Cooking Instructions:

1. Insert the Crisper Basket and close the hood. Select ROAST, set the temperature to 360°F (182°C), and set the time to 10 minutes.

2. Select START/STOP to start preheating. In a medium bowl, combine the soy sauce and honey. Spritz the Crisper Basket with cooking spray.

3. Add the cod in the basket, brush with the soy mixture, and sprinkle sesame seeds on top. Close the hood.

4. ROAST for 7 to 9 minutes, or until heated through. Transfer the fish on a wire rack to cool for a couple of minutes before serving.

5. Serve and enjoy!

Fish Tacos

Preparation time: 15 minutes

Cook time: 9 to 12 minutes

Total time: 27 minutes

Serves: 4

Ingredients:

- 1 lb. white fish fillets
- ⅓ cup low-fat Greek yogurt
- 4 soft low-sodium whole-wheat tortillas
- 2 tsp. olive oil
- 3 tbsp. freshly squeezed lemon juice, divided
- 1½ cups chopped red cabbage
- 1 large carrot, grated
- ½ cup low-sodium salsa

Cooking Instructions:

1. Insert the Crisper Basket and close the hood. Select AIR CRISP, set the temperature to 400°F (204°C), and set the time to 12 minutes.

2. Select START/STOP to start preheating. Sprinkle the fish with the olive oil and drizzle with 1 tbsp. of lemon juice.

3. Close the hood and AIR CRISP for 9 to 12 minutes, or until the fish are cooked through.

4. Add together the remaining 2 tbsp. of lemon juice, the red cabbage, carrot, salsa, and yogurt in a medium bowl.

5. Give everything a good mix to combine. When the fish is cooked, take it out from the Crisper Basket and break it up into large pieces.

6. Serve with tortillas, and the cabbage mixture.

7. Serve immediately and enjoy!

Salmon Patty Bites

Preparation time: 10 minutes

Cook time: 10 to 15 minutes

Total time: 25 minutes

Serves: 4

Ingredients:

- 4 (5-oz./ 142-g) cans pink salmon, skinless, boneless in water, drained
- 2 tbsp. parsley flakes
- 2 tsp. Old Bay seasoning
- 2 eggs, beaten
- 1 cup whole-wheat panko bread crumbs
- 4 tbsp. finely minced red bell pepper
- Cooking spray

Cooking Instructions:

1. Insert the Crisper Basket and close the hood. Select AIR CRISP, set the temperature to 360°F (182°C), and set the time to 15 minutes.

2. Select START/STOP to start preheating. Spritz the Crisper Basket lightly with cooking spray.

3. Add together the salmon, eggs, panko bread crumbs, red bell pepper, parsley flakes, and Old Bay seasoning in a medium bowl.

4. Give everything a good mix. Form the mixture into 20 balls. Arrange the salmon bites in the Crisper Basket in a single layer.

5. Spray with cooking spray. Close the hood and AIR CRISP for 10 to 15 minutes until crispy, shaking the basket few times for even cooking.

6. Serve and enjoy!

Orange Shrimp

Preparation time: 15 minutes

Cook time: 10 to 15 minutes

Total time: 30 minutes

Serves: 4

Ingredients:

- 1 lb. medium shrimp, peeled and deveined, with tails off
- ⅓ cup orange juice
- 3 tsp. minced garlic
- 1 tsp. Old Bay seasoning
- ¼ to ½ tsp. cayenne pepper
- Cooking spray

Cooking Instructions:

1. Add together the orange juice, garlic, Old Bay seasoning, and cayenne pepper in a medium bowl. Give everything a good mix.

2. Pat the shrimp dry with paper towels to absorb any excess water. Add the shrimp to the marinade and stir to evenly coat.

3. Cover and place in the refrigerator for at least 30 minutes. Insert the Crisper Basket and close the hood.

4. Select AIR CRISP, set the temperature to 400°F (204°C), and set the time to 15 minutes. Select START/STOP to start preheating.

5. Spray the Crisper Basket lightly with cooking spray. Add the shrimp into the Crisper Basket. Close the hood and AIR CRISP for 5 minutes.

6. Shake the basket and lightly spray with olive oil. AIR CRISP until the shrimp are opaque for additional 5 to 10 more minutes.

7. Serve and enjoy!

Cod Fingers

Preparation time: 10 minutes

Cook time: 12 minutes

Total time: 22 minutes

Serves: 4

Ingredients:

- 1 lb. (454 g) cod fillets, cut into 1-inch strips
- 2 eggs, beaten
- 2 tbsp. milk
- 2 cups flour
- 1 cup cornmeal
- 1 tsp. seafood seasoning
- Salt, to taste
- Black pepper, to taste
- 1 cup bread crumbs

Cooking Instructions:

1. Insert the Crisper Basket and close the hood. Select AIR CRISP, set the temperature to 400°F (204°C), and set the time to 12 minutes.

2. Select START/STOP to start preheating. In a medium bowl, beat the eggs with the milk. Whisk very well until combine.

3. In a separate bowl, combine together the flour, cornmeal, seafood seasoning, salt, and pepper. On a plate, add the bread crumbs.

4. Dip the cod strips, one at a time, in the flour mixture, then in the egg mixture, finally in the bread crumb to coat evenly.

5. Transfer the cod strips in the Crisper Basket. Close the hood and AIR CRISP for 12 minutes until crispy.

6. Place the cod strips to a paper towel-lined plate.

7. Serve warm and enjoy!

APPETIZER RECIPES
Air Fried Potatoes

Preparation time: 15 minutes

Cook time: 20 minutes

Total time: 35 minutes

Serves: 4

Ingredients:

- 2 lb. baby red potatoes, quartered
- 2 tbsp. extra-virgin olive oil
- ¼ cup dried onion flakes
- 1 tsp. dried rosemary
- ½ tsp. onion powder
- ½ tsp. garlic powder
- ¼ tsp. celery powder
- ¼ tsp. freshly ground black pepper
- ½ tsp. dried parsley
- ½ tsp. sea salt

Cooking Instructions:

1. Insert the Crisper Basket and close the hood. Select AIR CRISP, set the temperature to 390°F (199°C), and set the time to 20 minutes.

2. Select START/STOP to start preheating. In a medium bowl, combine all of the ingredients and toss until evenly coated.

3. Once the unit beeps, add the potatoes to the basket. Close the hood and AIR CRISP for 10 minutes. Shake the basket after 10 minutes.

4. Transfer the basket back in the unit and close the hood. After 10 minutes, check for desired crispness. Continue cooking for additional 5 minutes more, if desired.

5. Serve and enjoy!

Steak Fries

Preparation time: 10 minutes

Cook time: 20 minutes

Total time: 30 minutes

Serves: 5

Ingredients:

- 1 (28-oz.) bag frozen steak fries
- Sal, to taste
- Pepper, to taste
- ½ cup beef gravy
- 1 cup shredded Mozzarella cheese
- 2 scallions, green parts only, chopped
- Cooking spray

Cooking Instructions:

1. Insert the Crisper Basket and close the hood. Select AIR CRISP, set the temperature to 400°F (204°C), and set the time to 20 minutes.

2. Select START/STOP to start preheating. Transfer the frozen steak fries in the basket and close the hood.

3. AIR CRISP for 10 minutes. Shake the basket and lightly spray the fries with cooking spray. Sprinkle with salt and pepper.

4. AIR CRISP for more 8 minutes. Pour the beef gravy into a medium, microwave-safe bowl. Microwave for 30 seconds.

5. Sprinkle the fries with the cheese. Close the hood and AIR CRISP for more 2 minutes, until the cheese is melted.

6. Add the fries to a serving bowl and drizzle with gravy. Sprinkle the scallions on top for a green garnish.

7. Serve and enjoy!

Sweet Potato Chips

Preparation time: 15 minutes

Cook time: 8 to 10 hours

Makes: 1 cup

Ingredients:

- 1 sweet potato, peeled
- ½ tbsp. avocado oil
- ½ tsp. sea salt

Cooking Instructions:

1. Slice the sweet potato with a mandoline. In a medium bowl, toss the sweet potato slices with the oil until evenly coated. Season with the salt.

2. Transfer the sweet potato slices flat on the Crisper Basket. Arrange them in a single layer, without overcrowding.

3. Place the basket in the pot and close the hood. Select DEHYDRATE, set the temperature to 120°F (49°C), and set the time to 10 hours.

4. Select START/STOP to start preheating. After 8 hours, check for desired doneness. Continue dehydrating for additional 2 hours, if desired.

5. When cooking is done, take out the basket and place the sweet potato chips to an airtight container. Store at room temperature.

6. Serve and enjoy!

BBQ Chicken Pizza

Preparation time: 10 minutes

Cook time: 8 minutes

Total time: 18 minutes

Serves: 1

Ingredients:

- 1 piece naan bread
- ¼ cup Barbecue sauce
- ¼ cup shredded Monterrey Jack cheese
- ¼ cup shredded Mozzarella cheese
- ½ chicken herby sausage, sliced
- 2 tbsp. red onion, thinly sliced
- Chopped cilantro or parsley, for garnish
- Cooking spray

Cooking Instructions:

1. Insert the Crisper Basket and close the hood. Select AIR CRISP, set the temperature to 400°F (204°C), and set the time to 8 minutes.

2. Select START/STOP to start preheating. Spray the bottom of naan bread with cooking spray. Place the Crisper Basket in the pot.

3. Brush with the Barbecue sauce. Top with the cheeses, sausage, and finish with the red onion. Close the hood and AIR CRISP for 8 minutes until the cheese is melted.

4. Garnish with the chopped cilantro or parsley before slicing.

5. Serve and enjoy!

Cheese Sandwiches

Preparation time: 15 minutes

Cook time: 5 to 6 minutes

Total time: 20 minutes

Serves: 5

Ingredients:

- 8 oz. Brie
- 8 slices oat nut bread
- 1 large ripe pear, cored and cut into ½-inch-thick slices
- 2 tbsp. butter, melted

Cooking Instructions:

1. Select BAKE, set the temperature to 360°F (182°C), and set the time to 6 minutes. Select START/STOP to start preheating.

2. Make the sandwiches: Spread each of 4 slices of bread with ¼ of the Brie. Top with the pear slices and remaining 4 bread slices.

3. Brush the sandwich on each side with the melted butter. Transfer the sandwiches in a baking pan, working in batches.

4. Place the pan directly in the pot. Close the hood and BAKE for 5 to 6 minutes until the cheese is melted.

5. Repeat with the remaining sandwiches.

6. Serve hot and enjoy!

Prosciutto-Wrapped Asparagus

Preparation time: 10 minutes

Cook time: 16 to 24 minutes

Total time: 34 minutes

Serves: 6

Ingredients:

- 12 asparagus spears, trimmed
- 24 pieces thinly sliced prosciutto
- Cooking spray

Cooking Instructions:

1. Insert the Crisper Basket and close the hood. Select AIR CRISP, set the temperature to 360°F (182°C), and set the time to 4 minutes.

2. Select START/STOP to start preheating. Wrap each asparagus spear with 2 slices of prosciutto. Repeat the procedure with the remaining asparagus and prosciutto.

3. Spritz the Crisper Basket with cooking spray. Add the 2 to 3 bundles in the Crisper Basket. Close the hood and AIR CRISP for 4 minutes.

4. Repeat the procedure with the rest of asparagus bundles. Transfer the bundles on a wire rack to cool for a couple of minutes.

5. Serve and enjoy!

Kale Chips

Preparation time: 10 minutes

Cook time: 8 to 12 minutes

Total time: 22 minutes

Serves: 4

Ingredients:

- 5 cups kale, large stems removed and chopped
- 2 tsp. canola oil
- ¼ tsp. smoked paprika
- ¼ tsp. kosher salt
- Cooking spray

Cooking Instructions:

1. Insert the Crisper Basket and close the hood. Select AIR CRISP, set the temperature to 390°F (199°C), and set the time to 6 minutes.

2. Select START/STOP to start preheating. Add together the kale, canola oil, smoked paprika, and kosher salt.

3. Spritz the Crisper Basket with cooking spray. Add half the kale in the Crisper Basket and close the hood.

4. AIR CRISP for 2 to 3 minutes. Shake the basket and AIR CRISP for additional 2 to 3 minutes, or until crispy.

5. Repeat the procedure with the remaining kale. Transfer the kale on a wire rack and allow to cool for a couple of minutes before serving.

6. Serve and enjoy!

Cheesy Artichoke

Preparation time: 10 minutes

Cook time: 8 minutes

Total time: 18 minutes

Serves: 14

Ingredients:

- 14 whole artichoke hearts, packed in water
- 1 egg, beaten
- ½ cup all-purpose flour
- ⅓ cup panko bread crumbs
- 1 tsp. Italian seasoning
- Cooking spray

Cooking Instructions:

1. Insert the Crisper Basket and close the hood. Select AIR CRISP, set the temperature to 380°F (193°C), and set the time to 8 minutes.

2. Select START/STOP to start preheating. Squeeze excess water from the artichoke hearts and pat dry with a dry paper.

3. Beat the egg in a medium bowl. Add the flour in a separate bowl. In a third bowl, combine the bread crumbs and Italian seasoning, and give everything s good stir.

4. Spray the Crisper Basket with cooking spray. Dredge the artichoke hearts in the flour, then the egg, and then the bread crumb mixture.

5. Transfer the breaded artichoke hearts in the Crisper Basket. Spray lightly with cooking spray.

6. Close the hood and AIR CRISP for 8 minutes, or until the artichoke turns brown, turning midway through the cooking.

7. Allow to cool for a couple of minutes before serving.

8. Serve and enjoy!

French Fries

Preparation time: 10 minutes

Cook time: 25 minutes

Total time: 35 minutes

Serves: 4

Ingredients:

- 1 lb. russet or Idaho potatoes, cut in 2-inch strips
- 3 tbsp. canola oil

Cooking Instructions:

1. In a medium bowl, add the potatoes and pour enough cold water to cover. Allow the potatoes to soak for about 30 minutes.

2. Drain the potatoes and pat dry with paper towel. Insert the Crisper Basket and close the hood.

3. Select AIR CRISP, set the temperature to 390°F (199°C), and set the time to 25 minutes. Select START/STOP to start preheating.

4. Toss the potatoes with the oil in another bowl. Once the unit beeps, add the potatoes to the basket. Close the hood and AIR CRISP for 10 minutes.

5. After 10 minutes, shake the basket well. Add the basket back in the unit and close the hood. After 10 minutes, check for desired crispness.

6. Cook for additional 5 minutes, if desired.

7. Serve with your favorite dipping sauce.

DESSERT RECIPES
Chocolate S'mores

Preparation time: 10 minutes

Cook time: 3 minutes

Total time: 13 minutes

Serves: 12

Ingredients:

- 12 whole cinnamon graham crackers
- 2 (1.55-oz. / 44-g) chocolate bars, broken into 12 pieces
- 12 marshmallows

Cooking Instructions:

1. Insert the Crisper Basket and close the hood. Select BAKE, set the temperature to 350°F (177°C), and set the time to 3 minutes.

2. Select START/STOP to start preheating. Halve each graham cracker into 2 squares. Add 6 graham cracker squares in the basket.

3. Add a piece of chocolate into each. Close the hood and BAKE for 2 minutes. Open the grill and add a marshmallow onto each piece of melted chocolate.

4. Bake for more 1 minute. Transfer the cooked s'mores from the grill to a serving bowl. Repeat the procedure for the rest of the 6 s'mores.

5. Top with the remaining graham cracker squares. Serve and enjoy!

Apple Crisp

Preparation time: 15 minutes

Cook time: 20 minutes

Total time: 35 minutes

Serves: 6

Ingredients:

- ½ lb. apples, cored and chopped
- ½ lb. pears, cored and chopped
- 1 cup flour
- 1 cup sugar
- 1 tbsp. butter
- 1 tsp. ground cinnamon
- ¼ tsp. ground cloves
- 1 tsp. vanilla extract
- ¼ cup chopped walnuts
- Whipped cream, for serving

Cooking Instructions:

1. Select BAKE, set the temperature to 340°F (171°C), and set the time to 20 minutes. Select START/STOP to start preheating.

2. Add the apples and pear in a greased baking pan. In a medium bowl, combine the remaining ingredients, except the walnuts and the whipped cream, until it forms a crumbles texture.

3. Pour the mixture over the fruits and spread it evenly. Top with the chopped walnuts. Place the pan directly in the pot.

4. Close the hood and BAKE for 20 minutes or until the top turns golden brown. Serve with whipped cream and enjoy!

Lemon Ricotta Cake

Preparation time: 10 minutes

Cook time: 25 minutes

Total time: 35 minutes

Serves: 6

Ingredients:

- 17.5 oz. ricotta cheese
- 5.4 oz. sugar
- 3 eggs, beaten
- 3 tbsp. flour
- 1 lemon, juiced and zested
- 2 tsp. vanilla extract

Cooking Instructions:

1. Select BAKE, set the temperature to 320°F (160°C), and set the time to 25 minutes. Select START/STOP to start preheating.

2. Combine all the ingredients in a medium bowl until a creamy consistency is achieved. Pour the mixture into a baking pan.

3. Place the pan directly in the pot. Close the hood and BAKE for 25 minutes or until a toothpick inserted in the center comes out clean.

4. Let to cool for a couple of minutes on a wire rack before serving.

5. Serve and enjoy!

Chocolate Bread Pudding

Preparation time: 15 minutes

Cook time: 10 to 12 minutes

Total time: 27 minutes

Serves: 8

Ingredients:

- 1 egg, beaten
- 1 egg yolk
- 2 tbsp. cocoa powder
- 1 tsp. vanilla
- 5 slices firm white bread, cubed
- ¾ cup chocolate milk
- 3 tbsp. brown sugar
- 3 tbsp. peanut butter
- Nonstick cooking spray

Cooking Instructions:

1. Select BAKE, set the temperature to 330°F (166°C), and set the time to 12 minutes. Select START/STOP to start preheating.

2. Spray a baking pan with nonstick cooking spray. In a medium bowl, add together the egg, egg yolk, chocolate milk, brown sugar, peanut butter, cocoa powder, and vanilla.

3. Whisk the ingredients until well combined. Fold in the bread cubes and give everything a good stir to mix.

4. Let the bread to soak for about 10 minutes. When ready, pour the egg mixture to the prepared baking pan.

5. Place the pan directly in the pot. Close the hood and BAKE for 10 to 12 minutes, or until the pudding is just firm to the touch.

6. Serve and enjoy!

Chia Pudding

Preparation time: 10 minutes

Cook time: 4 minutes

Total time: 14 minutes

Serves: 2

Ingredients:

- 1 cup chia seeds
- 1 cup unsweetened coconut milk
- 1 tsp. liquid stevia
- 1 tbsp. coconut oil
- 1 tsp. butter, melted

Cooking Instructions:

1. Select BAKE, set the temperature to 360°F (182°C), and set the time to 4 minutes. Select START/STOP to start preheating.

2. In a medium bowl, combine together the chia seeds, coconut milk, and stevia. Add the coconut oil and melted butter.

3. Give everything a good stir until well blended. Divide the mixture evenly between the ramekins, filling only about ⅔ of the way.

4. Transfer to the pot. Close the hood and BAKE for 4 minutes. Let to cool for a couple of minutes before serving.

5. Serve and enjoy!

Cinnamon Candied Apples

Preparation time: 10 minutes

Cook time: 12 minutes

Total time: 22 minutes

Serves: 4

Ingredients:

- 2 small Granny Smith apples, peeled and diced
- 1 cup packed light brown sugar
- 2 tsp. ground cinnamon

Cooking Instructions:

1. Select BAKE, set the temperature to 350°F (177°C), and set the time to 12 minutes. Select START/STOP to start preheating.

2. In a medium bowl, combine together the brown sugar and cinnamon. Add the apples to the bowl and stir until well coated.

3. Place the apples to a baking pan. Place the pan directly in the pot. Close the hood and BAKE for 9 minutes.

4. Stir the apples once and bake for more 3 minutes until softened.

5. Serve hot and enjoy!

Chocolate Pecan Pie

Preparation time: 10 minutes

Cook time: 25 minutes

Total time: 35 minutes

Serves: 8

Ingredients:

- 1 (9-inch) unbaked pie crust

Filling:

- 2 large eggs
- ⅓ cup butter, melted
- 1 cup sugar
- ½ cup all-purpose flour
- 1 cup milk chocolate chips
- 1½ cups coarsely chopped pecans
- 2 tbsp. bourbon

Cooking Instructions:

1. Select BAKE, set the temperature to 350°F (177°C), and set the time to 25 minutes. Select START/STOP to start preheating.

2. In a medium bowl, whisk the eggs and melted butter until creamy. Add the sugar and flour and give everything a good stir.

3. Mix in the milk chocolate chips, pecans, and bourbon and stir until well combined. Use a fork to prick holes in the bottom and sides of the pie crust.

4. Pour the prepared filling into the pie crust. Place the pie crust in the pot. Close the hood and BAKE for 25 minutes or until a toothpick inserted in the center comes out clean.

5. Let the pie cool for a couple of minutes in the basket before serving.

6. Serve and enjoy!

Coconut Chocolate Cake

Preparation time: 10 minutes

Cook time: 15 minutes

Total time: 25 minutes

Serves: 10

Ingredients:

- 1¼ cups unsweetened bakers' chocolate
- 1 stick butter
- 1 tsp. liquid stevia
- ⅓ cup shredded coconut
- 2 tbsp. coconut milk
- 2 eggs, beaten
- Cooking spray

Cooking Instructions:

1. Select BAKE, set the temperature to 330°F (166°C), and set the time to 15 minutes. Select START/STOP to start preheating.

2. Spray a baking pan with cooking spray. Add the chocolate, butter, and stevia in a microwave-safe bowl. Microwave for about 30 seconds until melted.

3. Allow the chocolate mixture cool to room temperature. Add the rest of the ingredients to the chocolate mixture.

4. Give everything a good stir until well incorporated. Pour the batter into the prepared baking pan. Place the pan directly in the pot.

5. Close the hood and BAKE for 15 minutes, or until a toothpick inserted in the center comes out clean. Remove from the pan.

6. Let to cool for a couple of minutes before serving.

7. Serve and enjoy!

Blueberry Cobbler

Preparation time: 10 minutes

Cook time: 30 minutes

Total time: 40 minutes

Serves: 6

Ingredients:

- 4 cups fresh blueberries
- 2 tsp. baking powder
- ¼ tsp. salt
- 6 tbsp. unsalted butter
- ¾ cup whole milk
- 1 tsp. grated lemon zest
- 1 cup sugar, plus 2 tbsp.
- 1 cup all-purpose flour, plus 2 tbsp.
- Juice of 1 lemon
- ⅛ tsp. ground cinnamon

Cooking Instructions:

1. Combine together the blueberries, lemon zest, 2 tablespoons of sugar, 2 tbsp. of flour, and lemon juice in a medium bowl.

2. In another bowl, combine the remaining 1 cup of flour and 1 cup of sugar, baking powder, and salt. Cut the butter into the flour mixture until it forms an even crumb texture.

3. Stir in the milk until a dough forms. Select BAKE, set the temperature to 350°F (177°C), and set the time to 30 minutes.

4. Select START/STOP to start preheating. Add the blueberry mixture into the baking pan, spreading it evenly across the pan.

5. Slowly pour the batter over the blueberry mixture, then sprinkle the cinnamon over the top. Once the unit beeps, place the pan directly in the pot.

6. Close the hood and BAKE for 30 minutes, until lightly golden. When cooking is complete, serve warm and enjoy!

www.ingramcontent.com/pod-product-compliance
Ingram Content Group UK Ltd.
Pitfield, Milton Keynes, MK11 3LW, UK
UKHW010659100325
4924UKWH00035B/501